John Welch

Also by John Welch

And Ada Ann

Out Walking

Blood and Dreams

Greeting Want

as editor:

Stories from South Asia

The Eastern Boroughs

John Welch

Shearsman Books
2004

First published in the United Kingdom in 2004 by
Shearsman Books,
58 Velwell Road,
Exeter EX4 4LD.

http://www.shearsman.com/

ISBN 0-907562-43-4

Copyright © John Welch, 2004.
The right of John Welch to be identified as the author of this work has been asserted by him in accordance with the Copyrights, Designs and Patents Act of 1988. All rights reserved. No part of this publication may be reproduced, stored in a retrieval system, transmitted in any form or by any means, electronic, mechanical, photocopying, recording or otherwise, without the prior permission of the publisher.

Front-cover illustration by Amanda Welch, copyright © Amanda Welch, 2004. All rights reserved. Photograph of the author on the back cover copyright © John Welch, 2004.

Acknowledgements

Poems from this collection have appeared in the following magazines: *Agenda; Ambit; Fire; fragmente; Grosseteste Review; Navis; Oasis; Rialto; Scintilla; Shearsman; Tears in the Fence; Tenth Muse; Wallpaper; Workshop.*

'Thirst' first appeared in 'April Eye: Poems for Peter Riley'; 'Bungalow: La-Mer' first appeared in 'Poems for Roger Langley'.

Contents

one:

Art / Work	11
Chartres	12
Edge	13
Bungalow: 'La-Mer'	14
Out Walking, Again	16
Creature	17
Orfeo	18
It Was	20
Missing Plinth	21
Lanyon at St Ives	22
Exhibit	24
The Feelings	25
Authored	26
The Good Things	28
At the Centre	31
Deaf	34
Language Lesson	36
Dig	38
Collected	42
Family	44
Shores	45
Fathering	51

two: On An Island

The Dough Bowl	61
On Arran	66
Duddon Valley	68
Isle of Purbeck	69
On Sark	71
Estuary	80
The Lure	85
That Time, In France	90
Here	95

three: A Poor Am

The Sense Of It	99
Turning	113
Hunger and Thirst	114
Parented	116
Analysis	118
Lyric	119
The Moments	124
Launched	126
St Aignan	128
At Watch	129
Rose Mirror	130
The Eastern Boroughs	132
Gallery	137
Benign Tumour	138
Swift	139
Lake	140
Breathe, Then	142
I Is	144
Mirrored	145

one

ART / WORK

That's right, keep it moving.
We have seen the spring and not been impressed.

It is tedious
Buying food under the trees. When we have
Heaped up enough grain

We'll whisper the truth in banks
Scatter it on the water
His mouth is in the air –

We have taken him out of the city
Clutching credit cards. Our funeral
Rites are a matter of dignity,
Gold leaf on a watery grave.

CHARTRES

*Saw it just after the war – they'd taken out all the glass.
Looked rather good.*
     The Ambassador.

Encrusted language, high altar under snow
As if there were meaning without sign,
A word made stone, and waking
It helps us to be dressed in light
Such as hesitates on stone –
Yes this might settle the hours.
Imagine the sky a roof of glass.
Language will get us outside it,
A labial softness pressed
Against the hardness of teeth.
It is the animal part of speech,
A fattening – then all at once
The doors swing open in the house of silence,
The window-shutters folded back
Like ears. I can imagine
Being emptied into all that music
Such as might sing
Free the damaged
     half of me.

EDGE

The god has gone back under the waves
Uselessly uselessly trying to write his name –
Watch each one falter just before it breaks.
He left their irretrievable margin.
His were the eyes that saw the tilted land
Where a life was waiting for us.
It grows out of a sort of mist
And the new house built on the edge of the cliff,
With the traffic behind, is a palace of views,
An entire life lived inside inverted commas.
Walking up through a rain-soaked wood,
Its speckledy light effects, you reach the viewpoint.
You stand there waiting for the photograph,
Focussing on the too-much of it.
The water is an unusual sort of grey.
Someone made it look easy then disappeared
Who met with such a satisfying end,
But now the sun has come out,
And these are our defeats the sea is smiling with.

BUNGALOW: 'LA-MER'

This shallow box is made of glass and wood
To have a word in front of it.

It is as if the word
Were prelude to some other music,

Perhaps the distant, lifting edge
Of water that you can't quite see from here.

But the sea is not a house, and this one
Having two birds in front of it

Which could be gulls or pigeons,
Stone or plaster, and are painted white

Frames the distance with its word.
Once inside and seated

All in that gleaming grave together
Would silence be the best of us?

Out walking early I had thought of them
In their low-windowed house,

Being born each day into the sun
With each fresh waking, dewfall on a page

Until one day they'll slip away
And leave this name scorched on a piece of wood –

For the time being it simply lifts
Its puzzling hyphen.

Today we're headed for the shore, but this?
It brings us close but still it holds us off,

Feather of air, a dying breath
Confronting ocean fronted by a word.

OUT WALKING, AGAIN

In the City a stench of white hyacinths,
Monstrous-headed daffodils. A prison-shaped dream
Was the future, like a vista closing behind me
With a flourish. I'd resorted to vengeful watching.

Be seated now – the fat man
Sweats slightly eating his food as a punishment.
These diners, how squalid they look when seen from above
Perched above the ruins of a meal.

Shelves of whole cheeses are ranged in a window –
Their dense expectant silence,
The sum of these vestiges a vain crust of buildings.
There is so much inside an empty sculpted head

Where a man absents himself from himself
Even if it does taste of the open air.
In an empty landscape I remembered wanting,
Chatting with the sybil

But standing as close as this
They people the unpeopled air,
These knowing faces, then look up –
Sunlight's estrangement of the whole facade.

CREATURE

The creature has learned
To make itself music
Plucking and sawing
Away at the guts of itself.
Muzzle scraping the ground
It has learned to play with its mouth
In a special kind of a way,
Half-starved at evening here in a
City will learn to grow quiet.

ORFEO

Saying neither No nor Yes
And always hurried on like this
He travels toward birdsong
Through the cool draughts of air
Blown down here in damp gusts,

Passing the roots of trees
That have a hold on silence
Imagining he's roused
The one who slept down there.
This time he'll bring her back.

He'd gone to ground like lightning, down after
Something imagined in the after-dark,
That fearful thing, to make it sing.
Should he turn round now, what will he see
Mirroring an absence?

Nevertheless like Grandmother's Footsteps
He senses a quick light tread of statues
Behind him breaking into movement,
Each foot planted in silence.
"Was what I tried to conjure there already?

Down here I am given
Desire to drown in, darkness to dream myself.
I carry my body of work,
Taking it forward. It fills
The space that's closing up behind me."

And so, remembering days
Of waking early to float downstairs,
Words gathering round him like a press of quills –
Flight is the only answer, mastered
By the change, so he might move

Upwards and into a slow arrest of air
To be all watching.
Claws shrivelled with excitement
He'll try to find the one swaying perch
In all that blandness.

But can the bird ever
Recover its track, before
Scattering into an insect-flight of words?
One's circling in that dreadful hollow
He's coming out from now, it spirals

Upward into the moment.
His open arms extend into the silence.
"Being here I don't know what to say" –
So turns, to where she goes from him
And with that meaning marries half the sky.

IT WAS

in a painting. The way the light had
of falling just there
and, seeing how it was, you felt
it might start to make you happy.
Here are the three figures
who are turning towards each other,
in the drapery flow half-
seated and half-floating
and if they are all anchored
this is because of an arm
reaching out for and grasping
a jug. It is something quite personal,
a particular moment
but at the same time so
much out-there and not-you –
as if it is you are being reached
out, and about to touch
a concealed remoteness,
an otherness which becomes
you and so
by this oblique route
here I am being
found, at home in the world.

MISSING PLINTH

A litter of memorials –
Helicopter-like one hangs there
Shadowing an absence.
He'd crossed a city grown abruptly quiet.
The gallery was a dream-like warren of rooms.
There was only one painting somewhere inside.
Perhaps it was the one
Where the half-bandaged god
Was taken into the ground
And if he yelled in the beginning
It surely must have been for lack of self.
Now, hanging in that final room,
He wondered, is it this
That outlasts being devoured, all
Painted surface and its paradox of depth?
Aching, he rose from sleep and it was like
Being born again into the air
Turning to look back, one final time,
At the building, its facade
Lifted into the day's first light
And calm as the missing statue's brow.

LANYON AT ST IVES

There was this man, passionate about gliding, who fell out of the sky's silence and into the landscape he'd painted all his life – first a cracked vertebra, then a blood clot that tricked the brain and that was how he died. 'But I have always relied on some basic feeling of infinity', he wrote.

I look out over the deserted
January beach,
Watch the advancing crash
Of waves in brilliant sunshine.
Behind me are his paintings,
A line of them on their curve of wall.
There is the way this enormous curve of glass
Silences the sea out there.
Between it and the canvas
Is where for now I am,
The sea-theatre framed and a life
That stops at the frame.
I'd imagined that what I chose out there –
The pebble, the wave-worn wood –
Had chosen me. Not wasting a moment of being,
I'll breathe on the glass, to watch
The breath I am condensing there
While sea crawls up the beach
And it takes all afternoon.

He is somewhere here, at an angle to landscape
Under its final coating of sunlight.
Today such winter sun's a strength of shadow.
Moving aside to let the light pass
Where I go out into a fading afternoon
I pass closed galleries, out-of-season,
Walk through a gloom of municipal gardens
Still looking for him, the man who fell from the sky.

In the sculpture garden winter palm-tree's rattle –
I turn round, hearing the flap of wings,
Dove perched on the self-monument.

EXHIBIT

A terror of not being seen has flown to the walls.
The painting is what makes you notice an edge.
Its landscape froths greens and blues.
A divided self just stays
Splashing about in the colour shallows
As if it were walking around in an eye.
It makes an arch of colour
In Hoxton, a day in October two thousand and two
Whose conjunction of event – the sun,
Turning of the earth and cloud
Being moved by wind – have all combined
To make this patch of sunlight, coming in
From outside, slowly move
Over a landscape's painted silence.
For once I am thoroughly here
Where a piece of blue is the name of the sky.
Arriving in unlit corners of the self
It tried to make the world come real –
But 'I' is this epiphany of absence.
It stepped back when that moment
Called consciousness of self
Split me away. Still falling
I'll settle on the room's four final walls.

THE FEELINGS

You will know when it finally leaves you
Disappearing as if it folds up inside
Itself, turns into a sign.
Love made this thing.
Anger is also its name

And he remembered them out of his childhood
Or rather, as if they were
What he remembered remembering
He thought, the feelings were like
Animals – part familiar and part strange.

But still there was this
Miracle of the sign he'd found,
Substanceless yet inexplicably solid
And it could replace
So much of the world.

AUTHORED

Getting towards the end it is
The silences he hears grow round him
And something that comes knocking at the door –
It is that selfsame sense of lack
Gets closer with the insistence of rhyme.

Struggling back to where his past began
He'd tried to write himself into the story.
'I was the chosen one
In my coat of imaginary colours.'
Could it exist without the writing down?

He had found a way of not being near,
A mind looking after itself
Like the bird that whiles away time in the air.
'At this distance one can be serious',
Sending the words out there

But now it seems to come from further off
Like an echo in retreat,
A shout going distant in the afternoon.
As if dawdling on one foot art
Gave him the illusion of being,

'I' folded into 'you' and trying to find
A way to it, as the split tree's lightning self
Once held to that crack in the light.
It is as if he is filling the wound with sound
And something eaten day by day

In a perfect solitude resists
These steady encroachments of silence.
Now like a *kouros* there's something
Steps forward, one quiet foot leading
Out of the gathering emptiness: 'I am

What hovered by your shoulder
Attending to the page you held.
I'm moving round in front of you.
It's almost at an end
And you are my last hope of silence now.'

THE GOOD THINGS

The good things were
In there   but breath
It was cold on the pane
When he reached out writing his name there –

One of the first
Winters it was of being sent away –
And what he wrote, it was one more
Sign of an absence

But as if there were
A ripening   of the not-quite-visible
Or was it just the
Translation of an echo,

His life? He felt it was like
A novel of which he had never
Read more than the first few pages,
Such fullness of expectation

Being caught in the morning sunlight
And he could never quite bear to read more.
It is still there,
A book that waits all night beside its owner.

.

The good things, like
Berries in a frozen winter landscape,
Sun-flare on ice puddles –
It became a picture   ah those feelings.
He'll watch and watch

While 'now' is a photograph flooded with early light,
A pavement café, Atget, Paris 1930.
It is empty of people. Why is he drawn each
Day to this absence, sunlight on stone?
'I wrote the words on the way to somewhere.'
A child's hand reaching
Out and not quite finding

Imagined the glass cold as time
Laid over it –
Nostalgia was a name for it.

The book of 'he' – this
Particle might come to know
Itself
     out in the quiet rain.

.

The good things, he saw them.
They were in the exhibition.

These were desires
Gone to the walls,
There to take refuge in their frames.

Here was Christ in the garden,
Day breaking already
And he is back fresh from the earth
Painted in earth colours – 'Noli me tangere'.
He shrinks away
From the woman in the red skirt
Who is down on her knees and reaching forward.

Here is another,
His mouth a perfect O
As if the man in the painting
Were condemned like this to sing forever
And leave us to wonder
What we should do, out here, with his remains of sound.

The setting being 'The Artist's Room:
Rue du Cherche-midi' –
Bedstead, window and a small table.
But there are afternoons to nowhere,
Mute pressure on the page
That scarcely harms the paper,
The frame being home to someone
In the street of searching afternoon.

And later, seeing himself
Far out at sea – this was
Turner's 'Sea Monsters at Sunrise',
Light bundled up in the paint,
And where the light fell
On the picture, to join it
He was
So mysteriously *there*,
The watching-self as epilogue

Walking on through the exhibition
And their faces all looked
Out at him through the art.

AT THE CENTRE

A usual kind of paralysis
Installed here – is it compassion fatigue?
The years one spent in there,
Its administrative clatter,

The years of lost good causes.
Another meeting has been called
Sings the party of permanent government –
What meeting in a meeting?

These are the Minutes, read them, be unshriven
And how the live thing in you suffers
Open at its most tender part.
Maybe it's an illness I've subscribed to.

I came out, then I went back in,
Years spent climbing an endless staircase
Like an aural illusion, a note in music
That going up and up gets nowhere.

For half an hour or so perhaps I'll come
Closer to the one wish in your head.
We've each a code embedded into plastic.
The machine grows hot, all afternoon –

Which architect designed this mania,
Arranging pronouns in the social order?
Being privatised will hide behnd a logo
Even unto the air we breathe.

Post-modern are
Greek columns waxing lyrical in sunlight
Beside a half-emptied river,
Bitter the polluted air that eats them

Passing abandoned dockyards,
Extending to the city's river delta.
There was the one who always wore
His wound on the outside,

A suit of lights. He said
'This is the nothing I was meant to bring you'
But here consumer particles
Move all too quickly to be counted.

In a tower block beside a river
Just touched by morning sunlight
I imagine you learning the names
Scrawled on the walls there,

And, hot on the track of exile,
Is a voice weaving its way
Like the ghost of a refusal
Reflected in passing shop windows.

So we go on defined by our absences.
This is the shop windows' message,
The carefully chosen colours
That flare with a dry radiance.

Shortage, depletion,
Headlines manufacturing scarcity,
You are what you shall not have
Do you remember?

It was gold falling out of the sky,
Those trees blurred in a hot heavy wind
Engendered by the thrashing blades.
To what purpose? And then, this intoxication,

It crept along at ground level
In a haze of scented smoke, and the men
Who pass and who will not be recognised
Are the dream we endure, of the parcel recovered.

DEAF

The London Plane... believed to be of hybrid origin, a cross between the American and the Oriental Plane, or chenar... so prized was the shade of this tree that, when they transplanted it to France, the Romans extracted a 'solarium' by way of a tribute from any of the natives who should presume to put his head in its shade.

Isaac de Souza
From Goa, wearing a deaf-aid
Is on 'permanent supply' –

Would rather teach English,
Is still waiting to hear – perhaps
The Council's Disability Quota?

Or, paradoxically,
Will Equal Opportunities floor him
Since the job's not been properly advertised?
(There's no money to advertise it).

He can always unhook
The piece of plastic –
So deafness may have its uses.

Meanwhile I am picking over
The bones of this city
In one of its bleaker eastern suburbs.
The traffic is, well, traffic,
The maimed saplings we pass
A lesson to us all.

"I mean, I've been learning
This language for most of my life"
As he waits downstairs in the staffroom
For his timetable, in the school
Where I am teaching English
Both connoisseurs of
Impossible grammars
In the the plane-tree's, the chenar's shade.

LANGUAGE LESSON

Refugee trying to fasten
A red rose to the windscreen.

Grown in a greenhouse
It's not quite the colour of blood.

Enormous hidden populations,
City afloat on some sort of raft

But safe in here in here we're doing the language dance,
It's English as a Second Language

And that means I am in here
Teaching the words to do their best to find you.

When the time comes
To fix these words in your mouth

There is that space between us
And the language is like the news

Just before it reaches you.
It waits in the air, weighs down your bag.

This evening, walking down
A street whose rubbish blows towards us

Why should it resemble
The wasted landscape of a dream?

'In Turkey' you had told me
'History is difficult.

We have to learn the Sultans
Whose names all sound the same'.

You talked about Hikmet and you showed me
A greyish photograph – your father,

Some sort of Party gathering years ago
Somewhere near a lake and I had thought

The most of politics might be
An intelligent refusal

Watching your tower block subside
Into an effusive sunset.

DIG

The thing was to induce the vision of Portland Place to generalise itself. This is precisely the fashion however after which the prodigious city as I have called it does on occasion meet halfway those forms of intelligence of it that it recognises. All of which means that at a given moment the great Philistine vista would itself perform a miracle, would become interesting for a splendid atmospheric hour, as only London knows how, and that our business would be to understand it.
                              Henry James

Sir Leonard Woolley, archaeologist and excavator of Ur was born in a house on this site.
                    Plaque on a railway bridge in Hackney, East London.

Just opposite MC Breakers, Crash Repairs
As if the plaque announces someone waiting

To excavate silence, golden harp
Where birdsong tends a small wilderness.

But walking here, you might well ask
Where have they moved it to?

Here it's that inner-city mix
Of quasi-pastoral and light industrial,

A haze of leafage over blackish water
And the running children with their bright names.

Lives sifting down here are lived
At such a distance from the appalling centre

Where imagination falters
As figures jump over a screen –

Cuneiform flash, Sunday silence
In the City, another idea

That hides behind darkened window-glass.
It only reflects the briefest of passing selves.

The guard inside's half-sunk in shadow –
Enormous silence of a uniform.

Now walking away from the grave-plot of self
And all the voices in my head

I am limping into the future again.
Sundays like this are where the district wakes

As if greeting its own silences,
Ragwort, anchusa rising up through pavements,

June's squadrons of derelict roses,
Its pigeons doves that make the most of it.

It was something the light fell into
On afternoons of sun-shadowed

Architecture, when buildings take
Their bite out of time and in its museums

The perfect stillness of so much life
You cannot reach to through the brutal glass.

Outside again, the hurrying, suited
Figures cut out of the dark part of sunlight

Seem one-dimensional mostly,
Disappear as if into a photograph.

Or else apocalyptic
January sunshine, Camden Town

Lets say, in Royal College Street
Rimbaud's out walking with Verlaine.

There's architecture's suspension of time,
Oddness of these extraordinary terraces

As if once abandoned but now occupied
By a race of punctilious, anxious barbarians.

Here was archaic ground, sweat smell of grass,
Still rising from one mown and final field.

'One good fuck deserves another'
Said its goddess, afterwards

Lying back in those sublime muds,
Baked earth for building, writing

And they were coming in from the fields
Looking for money, filling the burial grounds.

I saw it once, the almost-promised city,
Wan streetlamps, idylls of rust.

This city, not a place exactly –
It was more a thing I'd balanced in my mind,

Crossed and recrossed by the absolute
Purity of bird flight.

Surrounded by the words to make me whole
I'd haunted its edge everywhere,

Discovered, I thought, the last indigene.
As if tricked into coming alive

And tracked to his favourite watering-hole
He was some words scrawled on a wall

Being just here, where
Language came to collide with the world.

Now they are talking and drinking, on the outer
Reaches of something nobody quite understands.

Had there been more words
I'm sure I might have found them

Like something abruptly come upon
In an empty square, clatter of pigeons' wings.

But as it was I simply went on walking,
Being filled with something that I could not name.

COLLECTED

The Collected was in
His glass-fronted bookcase,
My clergyman father
Who'd once quoted Prufrock
Standing there in the Vicarage study –
'No I am not Prince Hamlet
Nor was meant to be'. He had said it
With such sudden feeling.
For me there were to be later
More of these spectral encounters,
Stetson, the Fisher King
And the 'compound ghost's' baked features.
Somewhere between
My father and me
It was still there, the poem. It shimmered
Over a burnt-out landscape.
It makes me think of those
Pre-dawn epiphanies
Walking to early communion,
Or his day-trips to the country –
'Sempiternal' he wrote, 'though
Sodden towards sundown',
And today as I am passing
One of those huge London churches,
St Pancras, which was my grandfather's
Parish, and I was baptised there,
I dart abruptly in,
Smell that cinnamon and chrysanthemum smell,
A sense of being there and not-there
Among the flower-dust
And patient embroidery.

I have the bookcase now
Whose fringed shelves exhale
A polished mustiness
And I remember that gesture –
Him taking it down and handing it to me,
Eliot's Collected. Sometimes I feel
It was almost the only
Connection there was between us.
Being sixty years old I cannot
Help but start to imagine
Somewhere I might return to.
Hearing his voice that speaks, out of
A sort of hesitant stillness
I hover here, make myself other
Where reflections, branches and leaflight,
Like broken water are caught
In the bookcase's glass and the sunlight
Pours uselessly onto the page where I write.
My waste lands waited then
For impossible fertilities
And it is as if I'm still saying
Give me this, give me this, the
Love that blinds, and satisfies.

FAMILY

Whatever was it, the meaning
Of all that closeness, being at home together?
It's as if we were not sure
Quite what to do with it,
There was so much that went without saying
And I still find it hard to explain
The silences, surrounding us
Like pools of dusty light.
Today I found the pottery bowl,
The one I gave my father, a Christmas present,
When I was thirteen or so
As if it were my silence I was giving him
Inscribed with its puzzle of pattern.
I turn it round and round,
This object that is all
An openness and a containing
Watching the pattern shift and grow
And I remember the care
With which I went out by myself
And chose it, almost fifty years ago
On a fine December morning.

SHORES

The nightmare-withering,
   Something used up, then voided
In structures of rage.

You. Mouth
   Crying, in sand   ex-
tinction. The beautiful structures

That came to anchor limit,
   Far dome a
Presence in the mind.

So early in the
   Text it is
Light walks.

What reflection implies: this
   Stillness, the not-
Broken all-mothering gaze.

Being born it was required
   I think myself somewhat
Further into that glass –

Matter as the
   Reflection of nothing,
And moments to come, of such

Absolute strangeness
   As I am being taken out into the air.
The reflection stays.

How it was to be alive –
   A statue hesitating in a dream?
In your 'iris dream' you saw

This wonderful new flower.
   You put it in your mouth.
How could the whole thing fit, you wondered.

More other than stone or leaf
   Your face is between my hands.
Outside day climbs from nothing

And, like an afterthought, behind us
   This huge, shallow pool has spread
An entire carpet of reflections.

Will this other remember?
   It turns to us its face of absence.
Branches stiffen in the wind.

Ours is the regular procession
   Each day like pilgrims
Through pine trees to a barren shore.

I remember how we once came
   Shorewards – and now a single sheet
Of water will suffice

To erase the
   Commerce we have
Had with this edge.

Tongue's brave in its salt armour,
   Full day on all our skins,
The names of water drying.

.

There is a sea-squirt
   Eats its brain
Having no further use for it.

Now here is a thing that I keep finding,
   Dried up fish thrown way inland.
It is like an emptied purse.

Here by this root I'll creep,
   My flesh a thing apart,
Pale branched standard

Naked-awkward and nowhere belonging.
   I'd carried an ache
Once buried in her careful weight

Until, not knowing when or how
   It was I would be fed
The world was brought to my lips

And appetite was found.
   Now sight I am now breath have come
Into the bay of her eyes.

Going right in,
   This stranger-cup
Warm boundary, becoming name.

Describing, world as
   Consolation
I am the oddness, flaw in the glass.

Plucked from the tree of names
   Are plants emerging from our patch of gravel,
Each raising its leaf, its flower.

Space being a 'perfect black body'
   There is heat-exchange all night long
Out at the end of the atmosphere

Where language takes me
   To an edge of nothing.
So on a night of perfect stillness

Air charged with water cools until,
   The dew-point reached, the table face
And chairs are pimpled with the drops,

This mirroring of nothing
   As intimate as a wet seat.
Next night we'll lean the chairs

Against the house
   To catch its stored-up heat
So that the seats stay dry.

·

I'll begin to invent the sea again.
   Single page is lonely knowledge.
Just caught by the departing wave

An edge of nothing
   Is taken back, into the planet's
Deep inward curve of matter.

I think I am as near
   As I shall ever be.
Each wave must surely heave itself

Into one final moment,
   A deckled edge and then
Our perfect page-like stillness.

I had a page, that listened
   To a movement of the wind,
All that blueness held

So easy in the embrasure of a window.
   I was with you in the emptiness.
Your stranger-nearness, now

This veil might lift
   Its cloud of signifiers. In there
A child's still swarming over

A breast. As if the food
   Being lifted to each mouth
Were to cry out its name.

Soustons, Southwest France

At the Victoria and Albert Museum

What can it mean, like this to
   Label a man Ocean?
This bloated head

Being fixed to a fountain floor,
   His office underneath these waters –
All its chairs are standing round

Never to be occupied.
   In such peculiar light
The wooden panels lift and stir.

Eventually I struggled out
   Past the quiet attendant
Into the bone-white light outside –

Poseidon still at my back
   What slow ascent, staircase of frozen waves,
Preposterous clerk to those waters.

FATHERING

At the Old Windmill, Gazely, Norfolk

A body – now it gives me
A particular strong earthy silence
And elements of sunrise

His frame being settled deep,
His portrait staring back
From seventy years ago

As if the light being
Glimpsed for the first time
The chemicals all bloomed.

Some inexplicable hope
Settled back onto that shiny surface.
No longer able to make speech

His smile still has an unused look.
It was as if he'd found
A way to put off living

And that was how death found him.
It used him quite suddenly,
A coin fresh-minted under ground.

Reflection   like a shoulder
In water, it heaves
Upward to a stilled surface.

It is someone there
Wanted the water deep
But now, a coming into breath,

Shoulder smeared with earth
Being stained with an agreement of sunrise –
He turned away to the sky.

.

The stars have broken out
Into their brutal glitter.
Frost-roughened trees

Lead up to a brick tower.
In there my children are asleep
Stacked one above the other.

In its doubt, its
Wakefulness seed stirs.
The year turns on its black heel.

As if it were being written
In the sleeping child,
(Can I sleep honestly?)

These fathers, battered
Antique medals'
Faint impress in the plush.

Years taller now,
The poem. Lies and whispers.
So it lasts, another lifetime.

.

Sperm-blink. The flesh is all I took
Away from such an act,

Little worm of light
Issuing across the border,

Secret serpent –
Have you the knack?

A line of light   you
Serpent-crept beneath a door.

Now child stand up,
I in my coat of many colours.

In light-array the
Want-serpent is battle-worn,

An open door the light-barrier
That once put me to flight.

.

Pheasant croak, faint
Roar of a two mile
Distant road.

These fathers I have found
Are what is this way coming,
Their breath-filled lightness is

A remoteness of being
Walking out over
Frozen December fields.

And now there are these five
Women, and one gaudy priest
Who calls himself a father –

A word made flesh
Has found its way to this
Raised heap of flint and brilliant glass.

Swelling in its window is
An easy blur of light.
It pauses, here on the floor

And how much of my childhood
Like this was stayed, withdrawn
Into such held-back watching.

In a dream I once made such a house,
Stone thing, container I contained
To grow inside, to look out over

The new fields growing
Grey with daybreak,
A self of buried rivers.

Yes, today I should wear myself like a leaf.

.

Early in my silence
At daybreak, scored by the sound

Of an aeroplane passing the world
The voice I am still tells it in my ear –

How a loving nature
Was frightened out of itself.

I go back to a heap of meaning.
My home has been such words

To construct an aching mirror
And take this tongue to hell.

But all that time an untouched thing
Was elsewhere looking after itself

And now the scar remembers
An ordinary hurt

Being what I have to show.
I'll weight it now towards you

And the scar fades to a tune.

Orchard: Upper Pant Farm, Gwent

What's bitten into is so cold
The flavour feels like something
Condensed out of October air.

Walking in your orchard –
Red Bramleys. Bending
To take them from the soaking grass,

Fruit of a fallen world.
A coming into breath is
Hearing the silence where I am

And the life of each leaf –
How it hangs still, before the fall.
It is something painfully clear.

Out here each fruit's a ripened brow
At daybreak, chilled with dew.
Our still-lives, being a meal withheld,

Are brought to table.
Each fruit is this
Perfected silence.

Self-portrait: Rembrandt at Kenwood

I walked across the Heath, and came
To this off-white dead house
One year later on a sunlit morning.

Finding the self-portrait, I
Being held by it, the look
Back at me's an indrawn breath

And the sun is at the window
Hiding the pigment with its radiance, where
Reflections jostle in its glass

So now it is my portrait, looking back
And full of all the unsaid things.
I am silent now,

A distant substance, fallen on by light.
The personal is so remote,
It is something found

The other side of all this hindering brightness,
A stranger-self that I might
Come upon, behind the years of

Pecking at the dome
Greeting myself at each return,
Each solitary epiphany.

It takes a life to shore it up.
No sooner reached it is abandoned
And then the sky dazzles, threshold of breath,

My hand on a doorknob of air.
Here I'm encountered, in hints and whispers.
This is the strangeness of the building

And what could I bring except my silent
Shield of recognition?
The face still watches in the dead house

For each lonely visitant.
The portrait's like a mask put on
Called 'consciousness of self'. Outside

I'll find myself in the rush of light,
The play of it on stone, on water
Until, it seems, I am:

Such radiant fortress.

After / Word, The Apology

The day: it draws me up at five,
First serious light
And I am trying not to put

That pious exhalation
Round an 'I', that
Thing like a faint nimbus.

These volumes all
Are only what I
Might have simply said

To each of you, there being
Simply the two of us.
It is our ordinary fame,

Still has an odd innocence –
Each time happened on it might
Be fresh and startling news.

It is a fallen world,
Blooms and moulds.
Mouth stuffed with petals

I exist the writing machine –
I am starting to dislike it,
This voice that comes off the page

And have walked
Through days of silence
Meaning to amend it.

two

On an Island

The Dough Bowl

North Cornwall
Late season and we are nearly at Land's End, the burnt grass a college of grasshoppers through the open bedroom window. The sculptor's house is like entering a cave, in a terrace of such – tin miner's cottages, and inside each room he has carefully repointed between the big irregular unplastered stones. All round are field-walls held together with ferns and grasses. The artists scatter to the fringe and the sculptor's daughter will one day, when a student of anthropology, write her dissertation on their community.

Walking down to Porthledden the first Sunday, down the valley and onto the rocky beach, a windy sunny evening. The sea's road made visible, a split trail in your head. You taste the sea from the cup of the sun. Each year trying to get closer, and you twisted your foot on the heel of rock.

Post-sixties immigrants, a dog called Goldmouth. Gimcrack villas and boarding houses, where damp gets in under sills like dirt under fingernails and curls the wood. 'Seacry', its rattling palms and its bosomy hydrangeas. Sea-holly at Sennen on the slope of dune and shallow cliff that slopes a long way back up to the car park, the flowers small thrones of intense blue, the leaves pale. At the edge of the waves a fringe of debris, fragments of seaweed and tiny scallop shells, slight pinks and oranges. The weather changes towards the end of the afternoon, a wall of darker sky leaning in from the horizon. People on the beach begin to move all over the enormous stretch of sand. Those staying in the whitening light grow paler, slower, more statuesque.

This is a scene that repeats itself; the young couple get out of their car, she is holding a handbag and totters awkwardly over the rough ground, he is fiddling with a complicated camera. She looks a bit bored, but pretends to be interested in a dutiful sort of way.

The abandoned tin mines are picturesque, can be savoured for their ghostliness. The girl in the craft shop talks about converting one of the most spectacular, right down on a rocky outcrop by the water, into a house. Mine chimneys; the riven stack. Walls of huge stones at Geevor like Inca ruins. The Cornishman who found the biggest nugget ever, in Australia. 'Welcome Stranger' – was that the name of a mine? Minerals / drugs / smuggling. Artists, romance, underdevelopment. Beatniks, St Ives and its painters. Du Maurier, Poldark; the tale, debased mythologies.

Going down the Cot Valley the sexual imagery of the cleft in the hill. Imagine him, the man who made love to a tree, caressing the wood of that delectable trunk, shiny but so firm, leaning right over it and it becomes something alive. He comes all over a small patch of moss. When you cross the bottom of the valley you go down ancient mossy steps and up the other side, harts tongue fern in all the crevices, and down to the beach at Cot – white boulders in afternoon sunlight, air and water edged with cold and children playing, end of summer and the feeling 'it can't last'.

The stone walls everywhere are intriguing because they are serviceable, nothing more, and dateless. Walking back over the top from Botallack to Cot, passing through a farm, our voices echo in the stone yard. St Just, over to the right now, the grey stone of the houses in pearly sunlight, level and still, field walls and some cows between us and the town; no sound except for noises of someone building a house behind us. You imagine a place safe from harm.

Lunchtime and a walk round St Just. Quietness of the stone, no trees. Huge Wesleyan chapel at the end of a very straight terrace; just round the corner a butcher's shop with a tiny shop window. It all reminded me of somewhere else – Italy? Narrow pathways between the back gardens of the terraces, patterns of chimneys, and the almost secret shops tucked away between the houses.

A picture called Afternoon. You are sitting in the living room, the rounded top of the sofa between you and the window and outside the montbretia in a great round clump, then the hedge, and beyond that the succession of cars, their tops just visible as they pass.

All round you are such careful ruined walls, such an accretion of departed lives. Single-mindedly you clear your way to the common and its vesture of greens and purples, heading towards Carynorth stone circle; seen from above, from the Carn, it looked like a pool in the lap of the hill, the stones rising out of gorse and heather. A hot morning, high-energy humming of bees. You lie inside the circle. Over on the other hill beyond the Carn the TV transmitter. Edited versions of the apocalypse to come. Parallels between that and the circle, both trapping and transmitting energies, visions. Simplicity of the act of raising the stones and setting them in a circle; a minimal alteration, but vital.

Early morning up the dew-wet track following the blaze of sun,

Each sensation separate and early.

Look back again at tended iron-age fields.

A yacht sleeps on the stretched ocean.

By midday, stare out of the circle, nothing but grass.

Sea wind and sun will polish you like a mirror.

 The church at Morvah, in an elbow of road,

Hayfields, the doze of sea:

Distant smells of animals and men.

Late afternoons of strong sunlight, dogs statuesque in the road.

A rooftop stained with lichen.

The midday page and the midnight page.

Connemara
The horizon gleams along the rail. Shearwaters dark over the water, knife-wings, legs too weak to stand on; gannets sliding past. Towns then that seem to just happen on the way to somewhere.

And on to here, stone walls against a bright sky, all the gaps showing, the stones not being fitted closely together. The way the houses are tucked in between the huge boulders. Small fields half-full of irises. A man walks up the unmade road and pauses by a small tree, two or three others stop there and talk, a sudden sense of what roads used to be like, a different scale and a sense of impending event.

Haymaking – one man with a tiny donkey pulling a tiny cart, making short journeys with loads of hay across the field. All the dark-suited old men dotted about the landscape, like punctuation marks. The owners of the house where we are staying are haymaking as well, all the family together with their horse and cart, the wife stamping the pile down.

I sit with J on the steps below the quay by the lagoon, watching the ternery across the water which is all a lake of light, birds diving in and out of this, heads twisting straight down as they hit the water with a great splash, and J is trying to distinguish between the different sorts, Sandwich Tern and Arctic Tern.

This landscape has a scoured, ancient look, the little bits of turf among the boulders. The blind, shuttered schoolhouse. I'm lying in a saucer of dunes, seeing nothing but blue sky and clouds all round when I look up. Amazing Prussian blue of the water further out (I remember the name of that colour from my paintbox when a child, it was the word intrigued me) when I get up and look at the sea, changing to a greeny-blue as the water gets shallower towards the beach. Looking back the rounded tops of the dunes are like miniature South Downs, horses feeding there. Certain fields, near the sea, are a complete thick carpet of flowers.

On another morning, coming down past the bridge and onto the beach, a sudden dazzle of whiteness off that very pale sand, the light-filled bowl of sky, blue sea and pale, fresh green of the dunes and a feeling of exaltation. Huge sweep of mountain with one tiny white house in the centre and just a few small fields rising behind it. A wall going straight up the hill; imagine them building it into the clouds.

V's simile, of a caterpillar she'd found, "Looks like he's wearing pyjamas." She said "Why isn't tomorrow now." For the first time, or so it seemed to me – she's three now – she said "It isn't fair". She wanted warm water to wash in, I said she couldn't have any, and she pointed that S, her brother, had just been washed in warm water.

There's a mad old man who lurks in the road, a thin wispy dark-suited figure with a soft white beard. Seizing bits of dock plant he waves them about admonishing the hedgerows.

The Dough Bowl
It was bought one wet afternoon in an English seaside town. Someone must have driven round Central Europe buying these things up, the light wood – limewood? – chiselled out by hand to make a wide, shallow bowl, and the marks this left have imparted a kind of shimmer to the surface. Acquiring it, it's as if you could buy someone else's hunger. I imagine it hanging on a wall, taking its bite out of time, something to return to and surrounding them with a sense of belonging, such as being fathered might. As well as the bowl I bought this enormous wooden ladle, and sitting inside the bowl now it looks more than ever like something out of a fairy tale. This summer we will head off once again for Europe's ragged fringes, reverse traffic moving from the centre to the edge. We'll scramble over hillsides covered in ruined terraces, thinking of the immense labour that went into their building as we watch those labouring figures where they dwindle in the fields like something seen through the wrong end of a telescope, and imagine what little we can see of ourselves in their lives, mirrors all around us turning black with time.

On Arran

This morning there is something
That drives me from my bed
To inhabit the shoreline quiet.
Earth's cover wastes.
Birds pick at it
Where it curls like a damp page.
There are pipits, insects,
And one seal's soapstone head
That's caught in a patch of sunlight.

Young guillemot, front
Smudged with oil –
It looked at first
As if it were nesting
In a tuft of grass
Till I got closer.
An eye black as oil
Flush with the head,
A neck that turns through
One hundred and eighty degrees.
Woven into the system
I am as quiet as the bird is
As the tide slaps closer, closer.

Over from Kintyre
Clouds rush to fill the morning.
Moving further across
The boulders, I am an awkward
Body now older
But on it a quick eye, to
Hook me here like a seed

As I move over this
Raised beach – for us, is it,
This stone and water garden?
I turn round to confront
Waves marching, in their pale of air
While from the red
Sandstone cliff there comes down
A curtain of blown water.
Finding a piece of wood
Dried feather-light as paper
I find I like this margin
Where the sea beds down in the grass.
This beach of boulders
Is pinkish, pale ochre, grey.
Plants colonise it
Existing here at the margin
Quite without visible means.
Silverweed has red threads
Extending among the stones.
There's orache, sowthistle,
Sandwort, wild beet,
Clumps of daisies
Above the cast-up lines of seaweed –
There's a line of green
A line of brown
A line of orange, and then
A stone wall I shall watch for ages.

Duddon Valley

On a day like this the furthest hills are blue
   Seem near. A friendly sucker
Waves in its warm pool of air.

Bracken races off up turning silver.
   The failure of description to supply the want,
To flesh it out and give it substance.

We seek confirmation among the boulders
   To anchor ourselves to their remote substance,
Pile cairns to mark the footpath story.

Everywhere information is verified.
   We look up the plants in the book,
The little red-haired sundew, the pure stonecrop.

Beside them garden flowers look blunted.
   There's the murmur of water.
 Now up on the mountain it's almost noon

And the sea, being twelve miles off
   Is a bar of blue.
Over it stands one cloud.

I imagine the life down there, cars
   Changing gear, a morning leaning
Forward into its press of traffic

And all at once being here I'm there
   Being caught at the head of the beach
In that rush of wind and sunlight.

Isle of Purbeck

Who has made the discovery of all this
On a day risen again without blemish.

I mean, today's
Stone-pale spring light

As if the quarry'd
Invaded the town.

"I have made up the single bed for you."
The landlady's brain-damaged daughter
Moans behind her door.
She is named after a flower
And the orange bedspread and curtains
Are a story everyone else has forgotten.

Chapman's pool   a still morning.
Empty bay behind me.
Here are such soft cliffs.
By these fossil-rich shales imagine
Landfall, across eye of water.
                              Today
The blackthorn is in full flower,
Makes a white track onto a crowded island.
Now I am walking between
This shelf of land and a nothing of sunlight
Reflected in water two hundred feet below.
Standing in front of the sea

I can hear the birds sing behind me
From a land of faded notices.
I watch how the small sail blends with the wind,
The faint stir far below
Of water over a pattern of seaweed.

Strolling at midnight
Below swelling balconies
Hearing the slop slop slop on the seawall.
Next day the brown heath
Trembled in a lens
Of heat, sails
Bellied round the point.

And reached an abandoned quarry
Like a temple set into the cliff.
I sprawled among fallen stone there
Then came around the point
To the Great Globe in the afternoon,
Where, on its shelf of garden,
Its absurd facts erode.

That voice   the place
Where *he* blends into *I*,
Pronominal interface,
The sky as border

Shrubs leaned out over this
Stretch of late-glittering water.
The tea-room was in a sort of Folly.
I went on down through a wood,
White Narcissus, faint-scented,
And as far as the beach.

In front of the bay's shallow curve
Crabs and lobsters were trapped
In a brick pool down on the Front.
They scuttled to the edge as if to shelter.
Mind and body both slowed leaning over
To watch, in the daze of late afternoon –
Such beautiful machines!

I stayed and stayed
Being so much here the tenant,
At last, of my own silence.

Isle of Purbeck, Dorset

On Sark

Island Notes
Anger   paranoia   aggression towards A   feeling of central 'blackness'.

A description of the room, description of the elements

The fridge
breathes gently
Cockcrow at 4AM

My dreams leak out and into a fellow sunrise, the rose transfer. The awful nightmare of laying everything waste in one outburst of savage violence. 'I' manoeuvres 'you' into impossible positions then strikes.

Gulls resting in the fields.
cockcrow to cockcrow, echoes
fuschias in tides
the sea in its rock temples,
tourists paying homage in their search for sand
a 'well-made poem'
children of drought – the work conceived in fear
a dark red up in the roof of the cave
sounds of voices, strung out across the road

deep in the well the eye of water
the 'I' of water
        and thou   a sea-grey day
the sea extends its influence over fields

All this sea-gazing, why? Desire for annihilation while sitting on a bench, 'In Memory . . . ?' My ILEA / gun dream, then anxiety lurking in the curtains.The man I met talking about rain – the way he kept hitting his fist against his palm. 2 middle-aged ladies, typical Sark holidaymakers.

The bay sinister and then cosy houses – all in miniature. Voices soft and insistent between the hedgerows. Innocent delight. Quarrelling in the rain. And for the first time that autumnal smell of the leaves after rain.

A's watercolours, postcards, my photos – and a few drawings I did as well? A large slow horse appears and disappears at a crossroads. No cars of course but the occasional tractor.

Recapturing innocence, as in certain forms of hunting (birdwatching, photography). Here. Greys and silvers on the sea, an evening of uncertain cloud, a single very faint gleam of sun.

Time is a room just near
seizing the day
but things become more *observed*, less a shaft going straight
                                                              through one.

Out at 9am, very quiet, a dazzle of sun on the sea over to the left and breeze like flickering eyelashes on the hedgerow and on the distant water. Sea very blue now over the tops of the hedges. Mill, church tower, and the Pilcher Monument, small but just visible, holding the skyline together. The Methodist cemetery, grass close-cropped, very plain stones worn and covered in lichen and mostly quite unreadable. Arranged in odd groups on the brown shoulder of turf, and in the distance a fragment of sea like a butterfly's wing. Thinking of the traditional folk dance we saw last time, the old men and women dressed up, moving slowly, the moves of the dance so often repeated – but why did it look like a rehearsal for something else?

The old silver mines, small chimneys rising above the bracken and here and there the spoil tips, whitish heaps still uncovered by any vegetation. Imagining silver bled out of the rock. Port à la Jument's in shadow but the kestrel hovering above us is in the sun, the sunlight showing through a speckled curtain of feathers. A solitary tern hitting the water then swerving back up a silvery fish held sideways in its beak. A raven being harried by a group of magpies above the bay. Cormorant, just its neck and bright yellow beak visible above the waves. Opened its beak very wide, then dived. A whole flock of them, around sixty, appeared round the headland and headed out over the sea. Where they settled on the water I could just make them out with the binoculars. Late sunlight in Dixcart wood, insects making a really loud humming, then suddenly all visible in the dusky light, suspended at different levels.

Just for a moment the words have a bloom on them, it could so easily fade

His phrase 'the bliss of ordinariness', is us in our lives

Ivy swarming with red admirals.

The occasional butterfly right down on the beach.

On an Island

Watching myself approach
The island: shavings of distance.

Beside a sunlit sea's
My depleted parentage –

It is what the sea has drowned
With its alphabet
          A ruined game

And here I am, perfect, with a stone to sit on.
Like a lens clearing
The memory
Airs itself, sailing away,
Will see me, where I dwindle
To a blade of grass.

Next day, the Islander –
Its going-away affairs droned overhead,
Archaic silver sky-stance.

Down here, the pleasures of free-wheeling!
Passing the pale hydrangea flares
Where fields verge into brightness.
What drifts across is dust or mist.
Beside the silver mines
We searched the whitish heaps of spoil.
A trace of habitation searched for –

A gate marked Private
Across a grassy lane. This watchful absence
Is what I shall become.

There are the others.
Now they squeeze past –
I'll let them go back the way they came.

Buff roads and high dust-whitened hedges
Hide conversations.
Barnacle galaxies on a face of rock.
Gull resting in a field.

The humble victories of sleep;
Cockcrow answering cockcrow.
The black snout of a fish
From under its lip of stone.

Anxiety, in a curtain, it hangs
There deprived.
The roof of the cave dark red, ferns growing up there,
Its mouth twice daily blocked by sea.
From the well the I of water, looks back up at me
A sea-grey day, its influence over fields.
Inland will equal
A pail of water dipped in sunlight

He and She, on the beach at Grande Greve,
Two stones soak up the last of the sunlight.
The relief of turning back, up to land, its
Leaf-quiet and habitation.

Sitting on a bench inscribed In Memory:
I stare out over water
Is there a reward for all this watching?

Abraded stones stirred
Comfortably, down on the beach

While somebody's transistor
Was wearing away the morning.

Mist blurs, impelled
By a righteous sun to brightness

Suffused with
Birdsong in rainsoaked fir trees

And a smell of the sea again,
The damp earth full of signals.

Your paints blend and run with water.
Stones get worn to a planetary roundness.

They lie like offerings. The tide
Swells up to a listening beach.

I imagined the books in a future
Distance, printing like the fern's shadow,
Ink all a darkness of flight
On a page that is whitened with sunlight. This was
In a house my presence neared,

Yet overgrown, empty,
A place of becoming and ending. My ears
Are stopped with wax against that perpetual silence.

So what remains, of all that distance?
Vivid scripture of its blue.

You come home from the island jeweller's
With an agate in a ring – dark stone

Infused with white, this
Cloud-like drift, its permanence

Where a shack door empties the wind
Noon practises its palmistry
On wavering shadows.

Houses set back from the cliff
Are full-face to afternoon sunlight.
The local star exhausts its strength.

Out on the headland
Gorse-pods crackle open in the heat.
Sea has a mirror's distance, nearness.
A hawk escapes my eyes' cover.

Over and over
He searches still –
A useless treasure.
My being that took
'You' for a name
Was your white body a thorn invaded
And shelters in water,
Sunlight in leaves,
Reflections massed at the point of meeting,
Dawdles on a bicycle:
It sees over hedges
The distance home

Swaying down to the
'Westerly dipping
Biotite-gneiss',

An angry work
Whose outcrops have cooled:
I pass Beau Regard's green shutters

Travel toward the sea.
Telephone wires soar and dip.
The water pours off its shelf.

I watch the birds on the wind.
Late afternoon, I come on my family
Like strangers out on the cliff.

We are dazzled standing beside
This memorial to the drowned sailors
In a feast of windy sunlight.

      Sark, Channel Islands

Estuary

The marriage of biographies,
Yours and mine. Our obstinate
Freedoms light up the hedges.

Insect-shimmer in low-lying fields
While back in a house of stone pages are turning
A volume of our smiles.
There are disused factories overgrown with grass,
A spoor of production up split concrete lanes.

A peculiar darkish light
That prevails, a yellow field to our left
Where the flowers ride
And our intercourse – your body still fairer,

Abruptly the sky
And then the estuary, its gathered pools

In favoured silence
Approaching their horizon.

The estuary, no
Footpath through its solitary wet.
The water turns and heads in now
Joining itself, in swirls of conversation –
Invades a mud bed with its prussian blue.
Crisp waves are filled with light –
It was a divine bed wind felt along
Where sea ran parallel to our voices.

The tide comes in at walking pace
A widening tongue of water
Bringing small fish, they don't
Swim so much as are carried
Along, drifting sideways, twitching.

The beach makes a crackling sound.
Bubbles rise in a froth.
Gulls are dots out on the level sea.

In rockpools the seaweed
Frond upon frond rises straight up
Steaming in the sun.

The sea licks the land
And the sands dazzle.

Turning landward the saltings
Are mounds of close grass
Threaded with channels.

Into this particoloured
Field of creation
We two moved
With caution,

Turned walked back
Into a bank of birdsong
Standing out some way in front
Of where the land fell away steeply
Blueish in haze.

In the egg, clearness –
It holds a dark speck.
The albumen clouds
To ripen in noisy woods.

．

Behind the dunes water captures
The bivalves, their opening tune.

Back in the town exploding on asphalt
Came a smell of the first fat raindrops.

For a long time
We went down lanes of conversation.
A factory glimmered in the haze.
The tide withdrew.
It left our voices chaired by wind
Which the sea takes up
Reflective in its air.
On the other side of the hill
I guess lips formed deftly for speech.
What I write is the distance,
'Dead ground' between here and the estuary –

Derelict farms,
Cemetery, waste-tip.
A train trundles across
Half-finished sentence I'm still gazing after,

Windless distance,
Points, on a line
Bursting with fractions,
A wafer of land
That's not sure where to go.

But just before you get there
You can smell water –

Going down there I'll take a look.

.

Or else the people
Whose ways are that bit foreign –

This factory, that
Fraying edge of cloud.
Likewise my torn verse,
Its blessing of disguise.

Enough to eat, but
Harder to read the ideas
Pierced by a flight of objects
Falling in a slow curve.

The town curdles
In a wide valley.
Shapeless in the cold
Lined faces
'Just like in Russia'.
DO IT ALL DIY

Suspended in the mirror
The driver's face looks small,
Chats up two girls as they get off.
We all hang over the valley
Its precipitous heaps of slag –
Surplus and spoil, waste ground,
Exchange of courtesies,

Houses along every ridge,
Bluffs of cold, worn outcrops
Where we have been and haven't.

MFI TESCO
Freshly turned banks of earth,
'Consumer durables' – imagine
One lit from all sides,
Lets say below that
Conifer-dark hill
And approached over long brown grass
To where it's resting just above the ground,
A meeting point of all these forces
It is both more and less than substance,
Hologram in a ruined valley.
Slowly the light of afternoon
Will spread and fill again.
The bus doors open with a sigh.

Back there the estuary's
Vague grass that rare birds fly among,
Remembering the factory –
A plundered temple
It floated in haze.

Llwnhendy / Swansea

The Lure

The river speaks an absence clearly –
I could not imitate
The accent if I tried.

Calls across
To the Ferry –
Warkworth Hermitage,

Its rock, and the
Boat's faint clatter.

Bird-call, from the dark
Late summer trees,
A stillness over water.

  This riven homage
Among the rock's dim thunder.

Shell of what I am saying, these
  Boats are bobbing –
    One seen now from way above, it
Drifts, without a companion.

Now I am stilled to an acquiescence:
A midday glare's on things.
Kingfisher   tropical blue
Over the black water.

He flew quite straight –
How his motion is
And not one bit like mine

Where waterlights are polishing the grey trunks.

Return to the river's mud-coloured sublime,
Its faintly dimpled cheek,
River all in shade.
The angler is wrapped in its calms, brings
A cloud of insects like dust in flight.
He came clambering over the stained
Boulders, in his suit of olive green,
Rod so fine and whippy, attenuate phallus,
The string bag his keep-net vagina.
Athletic sea-trout – watch it leaping
From this so calm surface, fracturing sunlight.
Does he know how the
Sexual lure spreads on the water?

Others watch birds, their faces screwed up
In an agony of looking, for that remote thing,
Fledged dinosaur, ominous: the elusive rarity,
Hung round with notebooks, maps and binoculars
Watching or reaching down, what will
Burst from the sky- or water-blankness?

What the sea burns off
In early rays,
Residuum of mist,
 Is like an explanation
That I did not try.
A valley fills with cars.

We'll drive out to the hills.
I'll read my future in a pool of liquor –
Black Forest Gateau
At the Tankerville Arms.

Between the opencast mine and the castle
Is a suburb of Thirties semis discreetly set
Away from the old town, and ours has
Walls hung with heavy papers, embossed
With an inscrutable pattern, extraordinary bright carpets,
Bowls, jugs, ashtrays and vases, surfeit of
Devices for holding things, every one empty.
A sort of winged easy chair, solid to the eye
Topples when you touch it, as do the porcelain
Taiwan ladies. Just across the field
Is the castle whose keep has
Locked rooms preserved for a local duke.
Everything will be preserved if not sanctified.

There will be a pageant, hence locals
In their motley streaming over
The cricket field at twilight –
Look, here's another one coming
In dressing gown and sandals.

So, to skirt all this,
At a watching distance
I look down, again at that slow water.
"The traveller, returning in the evening"

And I did not cross the river.
The ferryman – I only saw him once,
'English Heritage: No Private Boats To Land',
This being an island of notices.
Crossing the playing fields so I almost float
They gather to bowl to each other in the nets
Where courtesies of good evening still prevail
Like "some old print",
A bitterness of engravings...
I'll pick my way through it

But could not imitate
The accent if I tried.

The Tower
Some years before we had rented part of a large house near the village of C. in the same county. The house had been built around a mediaeval tower, fortified against raiders from across the border. The house was still lived in by the family who had been there for some hundreds of years. Their name was the same as the name of the village. In the village there was a small harbour, with a commemorative plaque saying it had been constructed by this family, in memory of one of its members who had been killed in the Tibetan Wars. The family had long-standing army connections and the part of the house we occupied was destined to become the home of one of them, currently serving in the army in Germany.

Just before the end of our stay we discovered we could get into the bottom part of the tower from our part of the house. You went through an outer and then an inner door. Over this inner door was a sign which read 'Attention! Passage of Members of Foreign Military Missions Prohibited.' This was repeated in French, German and Russian. It had been framed and a small brass plate on the frame read 'Major C. In Memory for Officially Sanctioning the Breaking of All These Signs.'

This door led into the tower itself, a high room with an arched ceiling. The floor was of enormous stones and very uneven. It was covered with a large area of spectral green mould, of a vivid emerald colour. In one corner stood a wooden chest. When opened it disclosed another chest of identical design. The label read 'Wenham Lake Ice Co.' – it was an early kind of refrigerator. A huge chain hung from the ceiling. There was one window and the embrasure revealed how massively thick the walls were – a good four feet. On the wall were two trophies; at one end a skull bearing a massive pair of antlers, and at the other an equally massive pair of buffalo horns. In their hugeness both had a primeval quality. Incongruously stuck to the wall, above the antlers, was a garish plastic Union Jack.

Northumberland

That Time, in France

En Route
A dream: at the cheese counter three elderly men all alarmingly vigorous, like scrawny babies. One has a knife and is threatening to stab the woman behind the counter with it – the knife, somebody says, is 'hot'. Behind the counter there's also a pallid, lifeless figure – it's a woman sculpted out of cheese. It's supposed to be my turn now but then a woman edges in front of me, taking my place in the queue, and now she has a bowl of something in front of her. I look down at it. "Enjoy your meal" I say savagely.

To the one who is hungry inside
It is all the child's fantasy
Of 'what is inside there?'
 All about what is me, what is not-me.
'I' is what has divided me
Where flesh once tore itself open.
To bring this about –
Night after night, how those two must have laboured!

France, it was
Nostalgia of the other life –
Parental honeymoon, Paris
In nineteen thirty nine.

Hotel
Jug, of such thick, heavy glass –
Breast? Belly? – had shattered.
In here I am floating above the carpet.
There are slivers lodged in its pile
And I'm thinking of – eating them?
                    HOTEL OLYMPIA
Signature of this dream.

The next night HOTEL BRISTOL
A name at rest on a rooftop.
It equalled sleep.
I thought of the special bodies of children
Each in its perfect envelope of skin
And finally 'I' dreamed well.

Andouillette
At the Comptoir de Paris
Where we were almost the only diners
'Tu sais, c'est les abats'
The young waitress said, and she
Rubbed her stomach.
Slicing the sausage
I watched the guts of it
Spill out, in a soft profusion.

Midday
'Closed for lunch': walk through
Impossibly faded towns,
Voices glimpsed behind shutters.

I am thinking, what is it doing,
The words trying to find it out?
Like a blind animal's claw

The reach, the sway
Into an emptiness of air,
A faint touch, the famished presence still

As if reaching out to tell.

At Mallenches
4.30 am is
Lying in bed
Watching sky come, breathes
Carefully, beside this breathing other.
It is no longer to get children
That we're sprawled here at noon
But as if flesh opened up
With its odd, self-emptying cry.

Now it is late afternoon
In a ditch of sleep
And there are several me's
Trying to climb out of here.

Yes that was a real You happened there,
An explosion into the landscape
Where it superintends the sun's glare.
While I was asleep beside the tumulus
(Who vomited up this spiral of stones?)
She offers a breast to the silence
While a bird goes up and down
Liquidly with its small song
And over Lozere the fraying edge of a storm.

The Bathing Place
A village can make its own kind of silence.
A cat watched us pass, he was
Perched at an edge of sky.
Scarcely a place it was

Scar on a hillside, heap of fallen stone,
Orchard of abandoned fruit
Grown heavy towards earth
As if what 'I' became was almost forgotten.

Here a defenceless awkwardness
Bathes itself in the
Water-lights – seeing them shine
On the undersides of boulders.

What odd hairless creatures we are,
Moving among the stones.
There's a moment of completeness
On leaving the water,

The body owning itself
In a play of light and shadow,
Is where you are being everywhere
As a breeze starts up the gorge.

The child so intent waist-deep through water,
So lightly she bears the weight of the world
And we go back up to the car,
Fossil-fuel dinosaur lumbering away.

To Resume
Time will abolish the colours.
To be at peace with the sign, it
Catches the work half-made
Statue where it lifts out of the water
                              sets it up

Toucher c'est salir   I saw
On a sculpture somewhere
                preserving the monument,
Or like
The faint inscription inside the dreamer's skull,
Hears how these columns are reaching up into air .
I remembered this in the cathedral.
We had entered the guts of the building
At le Puy – it was two days later –
And I found it, a dolmen slice,
Blank page of darkish stone,
Pierre des apparitions dites des fièvres.
There was some light that fell
Onto it through a window of plain glass
And I thought of the analysts's couch
And some god up there, an all-seeing absence.

But still the constant
Striving to be
Here if anywhere at all
                at Chartres
In the Gallery not much,
Soutine: 'The Artist's Hat and Brush
Donated by a former Mistress'.
A painting does have the appearance
Of being so much the guardian of silence.
Esplanade Barrouze like a roomful of trees
Breeze moss   cowbells and crucifix
Solidity of a world of objects
So carefully disposed   sit down among them
Almost as if in mourning –
Behind is the hotel
So carefully prepared for our departure.

                              Cevennes

Here

A pale, watery bloodstain on the sheet. This is something you have almost finished with – 'like the last of the sun in the sky', you said, 'before it goes'. We get up. The tide is out. I walk over tilted fields of split rock gleaming with water and pick up a stranded starfish. The suckers on one of the arms slowly extend and contract in the brightness like drops of light. Will it live? I put it back, approach the crumbling shales. Here there are fossils. I look up, hearing slight falls of rock, each like an abrupt whisper from way above me. The stone can be split, opening like the pages of a book to show the creature inside. I find ones that other collectors have discarded. A microlite passes overhead like a giant insect. It's as if what we make and do is all imitation, flapping around this composite thing called 'world' as if just arrived from somewhere else with our words or paints, cataloguing, indexing – and here come the Open University students, in yellow helmets and carrying clipboards. 'Take care where you step', the leader says and then they all look upward, being lectured to about the rock. A man walks past jubilant because of the lobster in his pail buried under a heap of seaweed. Moving on and looking back, and thinking, 'human' is so much like an epilogue, coming along afterwards – this looking, like scavenging, as we drift across the pools of light.

There cannot in the end be any explanation for happiness. Days of such strong seeing, in the abrupt end-of-summer light, irregular stain of love, and a brief smell of blood on the wind. In the church there were black boards propped against the wall covered in careful script, biblical texts copied out three hundred years before. I looked up through the window and there is the sky and down here the writing. I thought I'd go back when the tide was out and find more fossils. I smashed open a likely looking round stone I'd brought back, but there was nothing inside. I spread out what I had on the table. Ammonite glints. It's as if by choosing one of these I say, I am chosen. It is the act of choice that creates significance. And now the ones we both found, arranged with a careful inconsequence, make a stone family.

As if something happened, and you can never be quite sure what it was or when. Alone now in the midst of all this water and light-filled space, as if 'you' is simply the echo of that distant explosion. Yesterday out on the hill I thought, this 'seeing-emptiness' is what I have, as we moved on upwards, towards a brow of hill and the approaching clouds. There was something that joined the two halves, something that was neither of us. Summer coming to an end, as I walked back into the town, and where I paused on its edge I suddenly sniffed a coal fire, sensing a first gleam of cold. So much of us is an afterwards, closing around the moment: where 'there' equals you.

Staithes, North Yorkshire

three

A Poor Am

THE SENSE OF IT

It started with being alone in the house and a sensation of drowning in the November afternoon. Then the darkness moving in took possession of the page and I was sitting there as if transfixed by it. A smell of burning dust when I switched on the electric fire, and a sense of 'here I am', my hand suddenly busy in the fading light. Maybe it is all about distance; you moved in too close or else you were too far away, like a concertina opening and closing. I reach for the switch and turn on the light and here at my desk, beginning to write, the distance is just as it should be.

Is that it then, the writer holding on to his desk for all he's worth? 'You do not need to leave the house', writes Kafka. 'Remain at your table and listen. Do not listen, just wait. Do not even wait, be wholly still and alone. The world will present itself to you for its unmasking, it can do no other, in ecstasy it will writhe at your feet.'

Mile End Park early on a fine Saturday morning. Passing someone's front door as it opens into abrupt light. There is the light's arrival on stone, the sunlight's relentless epiphanies, and that small block over there painted blue against the sky's azure – trying to puzzle it out as if one were trying to unpick the sky. I look with that exceptional intentness waiting for the gaze to be filled, and I am ageing all the time. Because what's simply *seen* can be a moment of happiness. For example those brilliant blurs of light I can see in among the leaves that are starting to turn. It's the sun on the cars on the road beyond. I *know* that, but what I catch a glimpse of, being taken up with that screen in front of my eyes, appears to be something quite distinct from what I know is behind there and, clutched at, it's achieved just at the moment of letting go.

Here are these two in the park on a windless day. They are *solitary as statues*, two *echoing pillars of blood*. I make a note of it, while all round them the leafy residue is being swept into pyramids. Wind disturbs the reeds by the lake, and a dog is coming towards me, all that inordinate bounding. Out walking to quieten the self; it's about making my personal silence somewhere in the world and I start to imagine a single room, chair, table and bed, and the reader is the one I turn abruptly away from, the words like a glance thrown over my shoulder while I carry on like this, a walking to nowhere in particular. And you? As if the pronoun were a form of address to distance. It's the distance I am walking towards, as if in a slow hurry to be beside you. I imagine I am keeping you safe in me and, like the water full of silence, I'll carry your reflection home.

Going out on a fine Autumn morning before sitting down at my desk, and again I feel completely taken up with what I'm seeing. It's one of those times that often happen when I'm out walking, when everything seen seems remarkable and I am filled with a calm exhilaration, while following various trains of thought and stopping every so often to write something down. This sense of heightened awareness when I'm out like this, whether in a city or in the countryside; it switches on almost at once and it makes me think of Adrian Stokes' phrase 'the calm delirium of consciousness.' When it is going well I have a feeling that *everything means*. I can't say what it means, that doesn't seem to be the point. It simply means, it has that sense of fullness. As an infant might feel at the breast? But today on my way back – and this is something that happens on these expeditions, often just after I've turned back for home – I get agitated, carrying on an irritable dialogue in my head. It can be anything that sets it off; something I heard on the news before I came out, or the motorist who crashes the lights as I'm crossing the road. But what struck me this morning was that I didn't exactly lose the feeling I had earlier. It was still there, and as I looked out across the park there was an odd doubleness, as if I were looking around the edge of my irritableness and still able to apprehend that other way of seeing though now temporarily cut off from it. It's as if the part of me that 'sees' is other. There is this 'I' that is me moving through the day, and this other seeing which is there as well and which feels almost like a separate thing.

Daybreak: as if all night I had had a lover whose departure left me here making signs. All I did was to go to sleep in front of the sky – it was lifting up my head for an answer that began this damage. Am 'I' enough? Self-sick: sick of this self inhabiting a grievance. This 'I' that hears me, intermittent self-echo. Discarded roadside mirror, half-smashed, left outside the house like a self laid aside. Dream furniture. Am I the man who walked into a mirror – the blink of silver, was that 'I'? And being gone it leaves me here in an ecstasy of unbecoming, self like a remote roar such as you can sometimes hear on a Saturday afternoon coming from a distant stadium.

A world completely empty of us would in its way be perfection. But consciousness of self made this rift. Self settles into a scar over the cut consciousness made in the world. I brought it to where it brought me, and here it only wants itself. It looks for its sustenance everywhere; this 'I' – as if it were a split that I can peer out through, forcing it open. Is 'god' no more than this consciousness of self, an abrupt seizure? Imagine what it must have been like, the apocalyptic suddenness of its arrival. Maybe animals are the ones that chose not to but simply turned away; and the way they look back at us now, we don't know quite what to make of it.

The puppet-master says 'Here I am'. Is *he* the one that says *I*? People say things like 'I forgot myself', or 'I was beside myself.' The conscious-of-self me – I have a sense of it being tethered to me but I feel it might float away. There's that possibility, the 'out-of-the-body' experience. I exist apart from it, and in some inconceivable way 'I am'. I can't help pronouns, the you for instance that keeps watch in me – I've got my own personal stalker. Charging round the kitchen getting in a rage with it, this 'you' that keeps watching when *you* aren't there.

Looking and looking, and all this 'me' is something that hangs there, an invisible container suspended in the air; at this moment I am not exactly in it because there will always be a something separate that watches. The play of pronouns; the you which is also I. The pronoun's a being made known

– because being known by the other is to be made. Knowing this 'other' there is a moment of overwhelming strangeness, like a tear in the membrane and a fleeting sense of what it might be to be no more pronoun, but simply to be here, made and erased in one infinitesimal moment.

Times when I can contain what contains me. Surface-tension holds it, a brimmingness. There are the contents, and there is feeling content. I think of all those mornings walking out early on my own, being contained in my seeing. Happiness was a kind of purposeful self-containedness, a way of starting the day. Back at home there are moments of a wholly relaxed seeing; those patches of lichen for example glimpsed in a corner of the afternoon, a moment when self is abandoned, when what is seen is the always-there, that is, the not-me, not dependent on me. It is a seeing that is akin to forgetfulness, a moment of fruitful not-being that, paradoxically, enables being.

Catching sight of the painting across the gallery I sense a pleasure centre opening up very slowly and some way off, as if somewhere in the back of my solar plexus. 'I am the life', I wrote, 'that does not quite know itself, looking at paintings in a silent room'. Inhabiting a surface as it bends towards the light, the picture made in the light's bafflement. We look at so much colour lighting the threshold. We learn to moderate our desire standing here in front of its representation – if 'here' is where the mind is, a glassed-in presence and the painting a hovering between object and not. Between itself and not is a sort of hesitancy. It 'makes reference to the natural world'. There's a sound of rain falling on the gallery skylight. It is a 'special condition of the restlessness of matter' across where self trundled its pronoun – imagine coming down to it each morning, though a gateway of owning. To believe in it, the art life. Art, like a door closing where there is no building. It swings back and forth like a pub sign and the artist has left you his name attached to the wall like a small claw.

Constable's painting 'Weymouth Beach: Bowleaze Cove and Jordan Hill' shows a sweep of beach, a low hill rising in the distance with clouds fountaining up behind it and, to the left, a stretch of sea. 'The sand is represented by the unprimed canvas' reads the label next to the painting where it hangs in the National Gallery. In the centre of the painting is a tiny, distant figure with a stick, accompanied by two dogs. Sea, land and sky – does the figure unite them, pulling them together? Sitting at my desk I'd imagined setting out across the city as if to a *rendez-vous*. The painting waits there for me like a bench out on the cliff 'In memory'. The distant upright figure is like an 'I' in the centre of a page. How does it manage to sustain itself in all that space, inside the peculiar silence that a painting makes? The landscape, patched with its browns and its greens, wraps itself around him like a coat. If it were me I would be trying out phrases. What I find frustrating is that I can't tell whether he is moving towards me or moving away. Or is it the landscape moving him towards me while just in front of me, littering the foreground, the painter has placed this assortment of untroubled boulders?

The musician, his instrument and I made three. Music is simply the inevitability of silence, meanwhile something to please the air. Where the music starts is somewhere inside-not-inside me, in those odd corners of being where I am always waiting for myself. Come upon unexpectedly gives it a special quality, like the orchestra we heard rehearsing in the abbey. Music that gives the illusion of something completed; about loss and sustaining that loss until the final, fading moment of sound. Sitting in here listening, watching the light dispersed by the stained glass and spreading over the pale stone, I could just make out fossils in the stone, as if its surface were brushed with them.

Sheep grazing on the skyline, and the clouds inhabiting that brilliance. Winter sunlight has a special quality, faintly purplish tree trunks, and the shadows falling across the edge of an empty field look as if they've been combed out of the trees. Midday, the shadows fully occupied in keeping still. Then the sound of a small plane from the nearby airfield keeping company with the slowly moving clouds. Standing beside the estuary reaching across to the hills over there on the other side with some words I write them down in the notebook I always carry. Sometimes this 'reaching out' feels as if it starts from an odd anomalous sort of space between my arms, or a straining out from my solar plexus. A 'thinking-across' to those hills as if one were trying to make something come true. But presumably one could simply step back and let the world fill up again with itself. What would it be like to be here without words? To see it without writing it all down, but to remain firmly here, on the edge of that endlessness. I am: the gulf of being. There must have been a place where I was found, somewhere on the edge of silence, like that leafless tree. It was foliage against an empty sky that made me think of writing.

This 'self' – as if I were reading a not very adequate translation and seeing round the words I could just make out the original, where it busied itself with cooking, arranging flowers – as I watched one opened like the remains of an eye. Parents who released me into becoming and who are now air, 'together who'd soiled the monument'. This was a line that I couldn't let go of. A monument, its dates, going out to inspect it briefly, the self like a shadow falling across it. But what I used to like, back then, was the winter ruination of gardens, a blurred gaze of statuary, and I'd go back indoors, back through the rinsings of light and up to my room. Up there was a self pencilled in as if it were someone I almost knew; consciousness the language accident and the words that had half-found me, self edged with a voice. Now there is this other here. She goes out and I'm moving from room to room picking things up and putting them down, opening cupboards and drawers. It's this taking for granted that is so peculiar. Able to enjoy the other – it's something I want and we get on well enough. But this closeness, I never quite know what it is. Thirty years of it now and I still cannot get my head round it. 'You look baffled' the therapist said, 'that's the word that occurs to me when I think of you.' I know I like her being there for me to return to. A point of reference can also be a point of departure. All that time spent in analysis trying to break the spell. Sometimes I feel like a shape-shifter able to adapt to anyone's style.

My address to the analyst, an odd patch of silence – is that him over there? The good object is the one that knows when to stay silent. 'He finds, finally, an echo in that silence', I wrote. Am I to be spoken, here? There are the walls we need, to confirm our sense of being. We cover them with pictures, mirrors. But who is this man sitting on the other side of the room? One thing I am supposed to know, the distance between us is there and cannot be transgressed. So 'Doctor, here I am', as if my 'illness' is what I am. These fantasies lift themselves out of my head, almost as if they had a separate life of their own – I entertain them, I indulge them. But I do not quite recognise myself in them. And if I asked that piece of breathing silence over there a question? Well, I am equally silent now. That's a sort of agreement between us. As a rule it would never do to be sitting together in a room doing nothing but saying nothing either. The agreement is sealed with the money I hand over to him every few weeks. Briefly I fall asleep and dream. I wake and I hand him the dream. He hands it back. It's as if I am trying to get rid of a mirror, but he simply hands it back saying 'No, not that.' He says it's as if I am trying to keep him alive. Meanwhile I am finding that even in my dreams I can be plausible.

There's always this other who is addressed. Lover or deity – one and the same, this is the convention, whether it's St John of the Cross, Sufism, Tukaram or whatever. Yes but *who* is it being addressed? And what's his address? This putative lover, the 'not impossible she'. . . Because in the end perhaps the project is to become this other, to *become* Shiva. Beginning being must end in flesh, 'I' folding itself into 'you'; the self-small eyrie for looking out of, you and I two equal containers. Who contemplates selfhood, a mirrored fullness, all the limbs assembled. Stepping outside it all those selves ago, the simple object with its light and shade echoes my new-found solidity – for example this short, fat pillar in the street with its multiple stainings, criss-crossed with leaf-shadow. The distance was something not to be easily arrived at.

It went on like this for a long time. But then they started, these moments that would happen in my head. It was a sort of flickering, a few seconds of absolute strangeness as if I were about to be carried away somewhere. In a way it was quite exciting. But it would pass and I was left with a sense of 'Where was I?' Not *déjà vu* but *jamais vu*. There was as it turned out a reason this – it was that thing growing away in my head. Since my operation half the tumour is still there but these 'moments' have stopped. There are still times of course when I can't remember what I came into the room for, where I put this or that down, and other occasional moments of forgetting. All right, this happens to everyone, but it's got more noticeable recently, as if there are gaps, odd empty spaces in the world opening up somewhere just behind you. But actually this sensation is not always wholly unpleasant. It can feel as if you are setting down a burden. Because you feel 'you' is still here as if hovering at a certain distance from all this. Maybe this is how, increasingly, it will be, and that is what 'you' is, a sort of perpetual hovering.

I remember shouting a lot when I came round from the operation. My head did hurt, and the oddness of the catheter, as if someone were doing the pissing for you. A smiling face – it was the surgeon's number two – materialised by the bed, saying they thought that perhaps it wasn't malignant after all. Then a woman was saying 'paracetamol, morphine?' I remember the tiny prick like a bee-sting in my thigh. From there on it's all a jumble. I know I changed wards, and some of my things got lost in the process. But things get smoothed over again and here I am sitting in a plastic chair and the Filipino nurse is spraying water over me. 'Americans, motherfuckers', he'd said the night before, pointing at the film on the TV, which fortunately broke down soon after, so we didn't have to have it on all the time, and he told me about his girl friend – a surgeon he said, back in Manila. 'Later I'll take the staples out' – this was what had been holding my skull together. 'Tomorrow I'll wash your hair.' Which was wonderful after all that time – it had got all stiff.

They only got half the tumour out. 'We went in at the wrong angle' one of the surgeons said, death like the sun being looked at for a moment; then it all breaks up into this confusion of world, so much world and I remember when I went out in the street a few days afterwards this odd sense of a container that's carrying 'me' around, and I'm both of them, container and contained. After just four days I was able to go out and walk round the square with my wife. When I took my head out into the street and tried it there it still didn't look right, swollen and with a sort of loose bandage that kept slipping off. We'd go into Starbucks – there was a kind of sticky flapjack thing I'd started to like. I came out of hospital after eight days, the day after they had told me they'd got the lab results and it definitely wasn't malignant after all – before the operation they'd told me they thought it very likely was. When they told me it was all right after all I felt strange. It was like the night before the operation, when lying in my bed I felt I was *over there*, on the other side of the room. I was there as well as here, as if a part of me had turned round to watch. Perhaps you could do it just like that, like pressing a switch. Or maybe it was one of those auras when that something got its claws into me for a moment and I was being carried away somewhere. 'The wound has healed well' I remember them saying, and now all I can feel this peculiar ridge in my skull. The way one's skin keeps repeating itself. Some weeks after the operation my skin developed an inexplicable, maddening itchiness, as if it were trying to tell me 'Yes, you are still here, in this eccentric container.' And at night I had to keep waking up as if to make sure. Was I still fighting the anaesthetic? I'd go to my room, sit there drinking tea waiting for daylight. 'I' is a coming to that strangeness, somewhere at the heart of this a profound absence, and here simply the world. I'm something made of moments entirely, this voice of mine, and a home to all that strangeness.

'Near death experiences', being conscious of what is going on when you are not conscious, when you are, strictly speaking, 'dead'. Someone describes floating above it all and looking down on his body on the bed, the doctors and nurses desperately working away, trying to bring him back. 'What are doing up there? Come down at once!' Reading about it, it all seems oddly plausible. It's something to do with pronouns, the way you just feel tethered to them. I relate it now to an odd sort of half-memory I have of being able to fly when I was a child. I could raise myself above the ground and float along, down the stairs, turning right at the bottom, out through the door and into the garden. The point is that, for a time, it was so easy – all you had to do was press a button in your head and away you went.

Six months on and another MRI brain-scan, mine almost the first appointment of the day. I walked down from the Angel to the hospital through morning mist, got briefly lost in the hospital basement's corridors. Lying inside the machine, hearing the operator's distorted voice and that odd grinding booming sound I imagined an endless printout of my thoughts. Once released into the denseness of air and traffic, balancing my head on its stalk, it's as if there were this voice, this thing as odd as a mirror, a something that has the world in its eye and it's telling me 'You are still here'. With a kind of mad innocence it follows me around, like the Tempter saying 'It can all be yours, and you are the fragment in all this that sets the other fragments flying.' I'm not sure how it gets me from there to here. It sleeps like an animal, wakes me and now I'm carrying on up the street, across Southampton Row; approaching the British Museum. It's as if I reach in past its strict facade to a place where everything's made still. In here my watching's coupled with a wish to touch – this tilted figure perhaps, taken from a temple, her arms thrown back, unstoppable in a sculpted swirl of garments. Holding myself still I'm here as if for ever, watching her resume her headless flying.

After the scan I went back, and there I was standing in front of a picture of my brain. There was a blur which was it I think – it was a sort of shadow mixed up with the other shapes in there 'Your brain is looking much better', he said. 'Come back in a year.'

The Battle of Britain pilot whose stories I'd been reading was called John Llewelyn Rhys and he was shot down and killed in 1940. It was some time before I realised how similar the stories were. Time and time again the same ritual of crossing the tarmac, climbing into the cockpit and taking off. The weather might vary – states of weather are states of mind – but always once he's up there he's looking down from so far off at the landscape, and then something comes up to him, this other plane, it's coming at him firing away, and he is twisting and turning, frantically judging distances. But there was another paragraph in the Rhys book that struck me: 'I was gazing at the little villages sliding by, thatched and tree-bound in settled peacefulness. It seemed that in this scene there was not only a joyful sense of homecoming, but also an answer to all the striving in my nature. I thought of how, as a child, there was this sudden magic in ordinary things, this wonder in a known scene; how for no reason a flood of experience, almost indefinable, widened the narrow path of one's life.'

Come on, admit it now before it's too late. It has been going on for so long. Anyone else would have sorted it out years ago, but you do have this extraordinary persistence. Acceptance or rejection – there comes a point where it almost seems like the same thing. But you do have to decide. You imagine simply turning your back on it and walking away. Instead you stay, but what you call 'staying' isn't really that; what it is is a continual setting out and then turning back, and each time you turn back – not at the instant of turning back, but just afterwards – there is this burst of rage. It happens when you're out shopping, as you turn back for home. 'It's a bad habit, this', you think. 'It can't be doing my heart any good.' You think that possibly you will one day get out of this habit. You say, 'I really can't leave, for all sorts of reasons'. But that's not the point. The point is, can you stay? There is this extraordinary restlessness close to her at night, this edging away you feel deep inside you. Hence perhaps your repetitive flights into fantasy. You say, was it all a mistake? But maybe it was bound to be a mistake, the one mistake you really wanted and needed to make. You half-knew that as you were making it. 'Our inheritance of happiness' you wrote once, recalling a moment soon afterwards, when you'd gone away together and arrived at the place where you were staying, getting off the train very early in the morning, and you were walking up the road, a fine April morning, no one much about yet as you walked along hand in hand, feeling that companionable sense one feels at that hour with the handful of people up as early as you. But always there was this 'mistake', walking along beside you, or like something perched on your shoulder. 'Well, it is *my* mistake after all', you say. 'So I'd better hang on to it.' All around you couples are breaking up, but more and more everything they say begins to sound like a rationalisation. That moment you experienced earlier today, a sudden slight vertigo – you commented on it to her at the time. There is this meal that you sit down to together. Do you want some of it? It is what is between us. An odd expression that, because it means both itself and its opposite at the same time – suggesting what joins us as if in a sort of conspiracy and what separates us.

Sorting through old papers. For years I'd kept notes from work, when I was teaching – my own observations, children's writings (lots of these), an assortment of documents, minutes of meetings, articles and so on. I'd get them out sometimes and sort through them as if this act alone might be enough to make them cohere and form a complete narrative. Sorting through these odds and ends I found some notes I'd made that were quite different. I could just about remember writing them; what I had written and then crossed out went like this: 'And it was as if I moved out of an age-long sense of being trapped, not knowing how it had happened, and bits of myself I had forgotten or that lay buried became myself again and I turned round to greet you.' The Indian poet Kabir wrote: 'I saw my Lord with the eye of my heart. I asked him, "Who are you?" He answered "You"'. Lifting up the mirror I speak someone who speaks me: 'You are: therefore I am'.

It emerges, as if with something in its beak. Outside the clouds have stopped moving. 'He wrote in a number of different styles'. Now it's time to start pretending to be yourself. To pretend is to make a claim of course, as in 'The Great Pretender' by Conan Doyle, bought in a church jumble sale when I was seven. I wrote my name in it and 'Number One'; I decided it was going to be the first book in my library though I never actually read it – as if there was a sort of shadow falling across those print-speckled pages. In any case I was puzzled by 'children's literature'. It was as if I used to take the wrong things seriously. It's the unread ones that still perplex me and sometimes I feel like a house full of unread books, as if it's my job to look after them. At boarding school, starting to write, I was convinced the words were holding something back. Concealed in the library whole afternoons, the sunlight as if coming in to find me, I was baffled why it seemed necessary to begin all over again, like starting Latin the first time I was sent away. Holidays, when I focused on the all-too-much of it in my room upstairs. I'd wander from door to desk to window, watching myself as if searching in a mirror for a mask. There was something I had thought I could heal with words, and the sense of an ending I was waiting for, it was something written down in a script I couldn't quite decipher. A poem still feels like this, an entirely new way to begin, walking itself first thing in the morning over a floor patched with light as it takes me up to my room. I is the entry point, upright hyphen, not quite a joiner. Sometimes it goes out early, looking back up at the curtained silence of bedroom windows. Out walking, down to the river, heron's wing shadows the water – as I watch it slowly descends to station itself at the margin and I hesitate to the words. It's as if I had drawn back from some enormous distance inside me and I was finally dreaming myself awake. Perhaps I had made the stranger mine before it even had a name, and the mirror's impossible text, it's the part of me that's still trying to tell you. Afflictions of silence like watching a dancer and wanting to be all movement, consciousness something freakish – as if you had breathed on its glass and now there's this other who breathes slowly like you, and she fills the mirror with life. Here comes the shy photographer, watching a man tread carefully round himself. A stranger to being in words, I live what I am lived by. It exists me up to the end, like something worn on a sleeve. Now, waking early and coming up here to my room at the top of the house, the sky like something breathed on by light, I am still this shadowy claimant, wearing it like an alert badge, and glimpsed out of the corner of my eye there it is flying away, its beak intact.

TURNING

A particular moment on the stairs, a
turning movement, in which I
forget myself and in that
forgetting I almost remember.
Then the water, a downward-gushing of light.
My hands are in it like pale stalks
turning foreign and cold
for a moment, the mind bereft of itself
existing as something apart.
Shrubs outside are settling into the breeze.
There's the smell of the soap,
and the wind turns the trees again, their
green unapproachable in this dull light.
My life going on is a steady pressure
through the afternoon. There is
this elsewhere that remains unspoken
when on me, like an accent, the pronoun falls.

HUNGER AND THIRST

Her skirts of shadow –
She was an echo folded into sky.
I had come here
With my feelings to be plenty
But, being echo-lonely,
Was hollowed out to speak, and so became
The throat in all that flesh.

Now fruit is swollen by light:
Appetite's a blind
And famished presence.
Imprisoned here
My wholeness fades.

I am trying out my death in the flesh.
Its wrinkles are pleats of light
And here comes the child,
The one who brought famine
Home in a brightening mirror.

.

From so far back – a distant dress,
Its simple patterned folds.
So thirst is under cloth.

In an infant's mouth it was
Beginnings of a word
But fails in air, can't tell –
We must build upwards!

Being good at thirst gets older, it can walk in the sky.
The thirst was announced in deserts
Where it sat as if inside a mouth
Or hovering there was the answer to a mirage.

There are wells if you think them
Are days in the telling.
All this it is a translation
Of thirst's slow story passing into flesh
That had the cool warmth we'd waited on.
It is what we dreamed through thin hours.

But the well was sealed with imagining.
It returned a stone breast to the sky
Inset with small panels, a
Pictured happiness.

PARENTED

Somewhere between boredom and longing
Was where I'd felt I almost always was.
There was something that felt banished,
It moved to its place of watching and waiting
And still she was there
With that smile of an all-knowing mothering sadness
As if the light were singing in its grave.

Spring twilight, passers-by
Mere ciphers in the streets.
What the light finds it
Hides,
    My father walking into me.
Resemblance merges, fades
As if a text of self were being made.

I want to come to you, I'd said
From the most enormous distance
To be a visitor here,
Travelling shaft of light that
Pauses, for just a moment,
Faint twitch of a curtain, and then that slow
Gathering of sound as the
Car, parked outside, pulls away.

So who is it lives in there now
As if baffled by his own absences –
What is it lives
In the spaces between each mouthful?
Breathing it lifts
Another page

And I can see it now.
It is the writing-self,

Me-not-me, in that
Perfected circle's pool of light –
Left long enough in here, I thought
The books will all read themselves

And looking in there I saw him.
It was Tantalus feeding.

ANALYSIS

A mirror, it hung
In an empty house.
Being what there was
Between me and silence
Its monotonous glass
Was miles of nothing.
Approaching it
From one side, inching up carefully
Some tendrils of breath escaped me.
A tap gurgled. Sunlight paraded
Everywhere over a floor.
Statues hovered somewhere, the
Infuriating clouds
Were slowly moving off.
But what I am trying to remember is
How, swimming up towards me
Out of nowhere, once it
Borrowed my face for a moment.

Walking the endless streets since then
Where time and distance flow together
I lie in another town,
A different ceiling underneath my head.
The mirror's a plain man telling me.
He sits behind my shoulder.
His glass is harsh
    While I remember
How once I breathed, then wrote my name
On a blurred surface, solitary tracings.

LYRIC

Each one now comes
So prompt to the breath birth –
O heave me off, she'd said,
This mass of flesh
Pinioned to window glare

And all *I* would want
Is to feed here in quiet,
This part of me, it
Eats and cries
Remembering how the blood was there.

Being bitten all over with hunger –
Love is in my corner,
This my blamed body,
Its otherness has brought me here.
Listen: my hunting diamond,

The wildness of the animal
Is the sharpness of its feature,
The burnt child, this cinder child,
While kestrel hung
Like an asterisk, free-floating hoverer

Above the defeated town,
Its vegetation lurching out from brickwork
And buddleia smell after rainfall –
At rest here under the eaves of light
I'll arrive here in a small voice

Here in the city that I thought was mine,
Its bombsites where a black redstart sang
Where I found a scorched photograph.
Stories are told to bind up wounds.
But my archaic ink –

With all my words, as if
I wanted to buy something
To better this bruised lyric,
Lips and throat, the heart-shaped vowels
To take my voice back home.

.

Leaf-touch
To ground   more
Substance needed here,

In a brotherhood of the air
To watch colour settle
Down into the trees,

Bird-claw clutch and
So on out –
It is   to reach
An edge of text
              to
Taste the salt,
Brushing against her skin.

Then, that being done,
Lips complete the word.

.

What's gone, and now at large
Where lips complete the wound:
Tongue challenge

To speak the sky,
Be flooded with
An emptiness, as if

Such looked-for absence
Might become an answer.
And what can you bring back
Inside here, into the fortress,
Token of one such day?

Stone shell feather.

.

A body is all hollows, bow
Stretched in air, and air
An absence waiting.

It is the shape I
Hollow here in my region
Of silences, but you knowing

Me: split image healed,
A crack joined with gold like
Lightning into the porcelain,

This coldness is a limb
Afloat on something deep who are
The skin we have to endure.

.

Light-hang, our
Space. It is the over-
towering lily stasis

Upholds the pond –
A lover of nothing
Parades But

Lotus cock-jewel,
The garment swish of
Water parting.

Air snapped like a flag.
I was posted to nowhere.
I am written out of my depth into light

Whose threads congeal,
Being seed   made parting
So the air dries a page.

.

I stir, for you
And I have to trust the words
More than I trust myself.

On an evening of rainwet fractured light,
Sun-drops peopling each bush
We'll drive further into the valley

Where the quality of the late
Light is like a released ache,
Skin-near and the

Rooks lift from treetops.
The winds take their cries.
Each leaf is the sum of light

And I wonder what this to-be-
held might be, in our quiet house
Over against the fall of dark

THE MOMENTS

Birth-moment – was it then,
The time that I finally lost
My quality of perfect stillness?

And the strangeness of it, an
'Orientation towards existence'.
Being older now

Like the afternoon sunlight trapped in cities –
Cracked window of a self
As if consciousness were a trick of the light.

.

'The core of emptiness
Which is our own mortality.'
Sprung fresh from the void

Tree means, as if it were
Leaning out of itself
And onto its branch of sky.

Buddleia, its blossom's
Soft fracture, breaks
Out into our air

Here. It is the quick blur
You were made in, that moment of self.
A careful arrangement of detail

Might well be enough
Where brightness disappeared into brightness,
Infant drinking to contentment.

Salvia Turkestanica
The long bud's like a fallen tower,
It lies on the broad leaf, held in the twist of it
Till it raises itself – there's a shining
Of very pale purple that
Darkens slightly, then opens
Into its petals, a crowd of small hooks.
The thick stem gets dense with hairs
That carry a stickiness, smelling of sweat
But cut with a fruitiness, acrid and sweet together
When it withers and dies. I brush
Against it now in the late, dry garden.
The seed-pods raise their arms like outworn selves.
On days like this I
Can re-visit myself
Being roused to a dazzle of air
And I feel an emptiness
Opening up inside me,
Great shallow heart of existence.
It is being
Quietly in your life I can almost remember.

LAUNCHED

It was a narrow door
Like a coffin lid, and swung open –
Ahead were the tight stairs.

Climbed up
There and out into birdsong, it was
Suddenly cool in the upstairs air.

Yes, their room, it is something out in the sky
With a window that lifts like a lid.
My head peers out of there.

.

I am, being
Abruptly up
Above all of that –
The cushions of garden,
Rafts of blossom,

Wing-whirr and the
Throat-swelling sound of them –
Yes, these are different doves
That land one by one on the rooftop,
Loose scrabble, of claws on slates.

.

The giant
     Couple who are
Being found each to each
On their beds of dawn.
Beyond and outside is
The work of cloud,
It is steadily building –

Imagine: being
Freed to go
Up to that bed of daybreak
And its enormous white, being
I
  is what writes on that page

ST AIGNAN

Here where time erodes
Its least important angel

In the crypt, the quiet
Moulds waiting in the earth,

Is where this other angel grew
Across the ceiling's curve

And sounds outside that I imagine
Turning to substance

Remembering who it is, will
Take itself outside,

A poor am, clothed in flesh.

AT WATCH

So out quite early
With bird book and binoculars

To take a walk around himself.
Is that Start Point

Where a hawk sails its shadow
Of name across the cliff-face?

He thinks, this is such a day –
What can I do with my luck?

As the mind sails out and on to
That brightening water, it curves

Inward to where the plumages merge,
And now the names divide,

Each like a razor separating
Flesh from flesh on an opened page of sky.

Tethered to the cliff-edge and
Weighted with his book

He'll rehearse it yet again, the
Being thrown forward, plunge into the air.

It's time to go back down the hill
To his well-windowed house

In hope of meeting
A winged self coming.

ROSE MIRROR

Mirror sniffed its rose,
The flower of absolutely nothing.
'This is my reflection.
It is rooted in emptiness'.

A roofless building. Inside
The light's like flapping pages
And I have walked here dry as air.
I'd come here once to find my voice.

My flesh, being sailed
To a place of failing powers
Was a book that closed its own pages.
'Now it gets late', she is saying

As we sing the possible burdens.
Infinity houses the hours of us
And here I am still, one roughened
Voice come late to ground,

The god I watch shrunk to its metal
While she complains
Of a certain remoteness of feeling.
'You are too far from yourself',

Because I never see myself
Except a partial gleam.
Could I eat my way to the light?
It's still a long way there,

Us in the night and
We'll take away some of the light-stuff
From the dark place together
To freshen the sill

Where it falls, on stone and tree trunk
Or paints a facade with letters
And so it is one rain-dark summer day
As I'm watching words and how

They fade back into the screen,
A sort of reverse etching,
I imagine one final twist of the knob
That will bring us both into focus.

THE EASTERN BOROUGHS

Here I am, Leyton in summer
And the light has aged me. Spill
Anywhere out of this world

Just here on an edge of London sunlight,
The small quiet backs of houses.
I am so full of quiet

These dinner-hours of solo walking
And a Faustian bargain's made in Leyton –
Verweile dich du bist so schön.

That tree being substance of itself's
So compact in its foliage,
Its leaves the being of summer sky.

There is the work of being
And I had thought it was words
Here among the Eastern boroughs.

.

The sun comes palely in
And faces are
An innocence of expectation.

Hidden face of a lake.
I moved my name into the sun
Feeling an odd kind of happiness

As if sunlight wind and water
Had ruffled the surface of the paint
On tight-stretched canvas.

The fruit's a leaning to the lake,
Reflection like a kind of echo.
There is a retreat into music,

I being one for whom the act
Of reading early on became
A kind of absence.

'Like this I can grow, like a
Scar over myself', I had thought – and
'Is there enough inside me yet?'

Was this why, falling quite
Silent for a time
I fed stories in last night's dream

To the pale hungry girl inside me.
'This is quite a good thing I have found',
I'd told myself, safe in my silence.

Here I'll stay with the good things inside me
Where light embraces a threshold
And find an emptiness that is myself.

.

Is it that words build a silence
Like the fruit's dense flavour built from light?
Each Autumn I was being called

To what the winter sees
After the spectacle of leaf-fall
As if one by one they had gone

Back to their names and we were walking on air,
The crisp tread, a barely yielding
Springiness of surface.

I remember now, out walking
Into my waiting silences,
How the words when I first found them

Were flocking in libraries, something
Miraculous in their way
Of resting on the silent curve of a page.

.

The I of it is another, is both
Epiphany and absence –
The way it looks up from feeding, wiping its mouth,

It is an afterwards,
Something that goes on clearing and claiming distance
In the picture's painted absence.

Still I *was* there
A winged self stretched like light,
Pinned across the door.

Today out walking with you all
I have come into this noise
Of wind and water everywhere,

There is something caged that
Looks for itself out here,
Something quite huge and I want it to leave me.

Remains of a tree still flush with berries
Out on the empty hillside as if
It were standing a little apart from itself.

I am feeling around inside myself
For what might be the light.
Are you here enough in the dark to find me?

You, the speaking silence,
Are making the space familiar.
You'll make me in your eyes –

Flesh and blood   behind the curtain
Owns up to being real.
So I'll grow in becoming to the world.

.

The camera looked at Eurydice
Where she hid in the photograph's shade.
She was light's image burnt into silver,

Daguerrotype mirror the light went into –
I was there too, an
Image deposit, salts drying in air,

An ash afloat
On its small lake of light.
Image on all this shininess

Is reflection seeking its answer
Where light still writes
Its letters from the dead.

But I have flown myself out of here.
Pecking at the mirror
I dreamt my arrival,

One moment, that is, of perfect being,
Hesitant fortress
I'd said – as if sky eats its messenger.

A fall of curtains
Here and there over a life.
I'll climb into myself.

You might be there too, cloud
Mixed with sunshine
To make this food real.

GALLERY

This city – it is
The heartfelt pause of sunlight
Out there on a piece of shaped stone.
A shadow of writing
Darkens it like soot
And we are both the tenants
Of this. But I have taken
Myself away from you
This November afternoon
And now it's starting to get dark.
'Vase of Black Wine' is a title,
The picture tilting its silence towards me
As I wait for you to arrive.
There is a kind of hopefulness waits in your arms
Like a calm end for those of us
Who, wearing our prose selves
Will one day arrive
Separate, but together
Each clothed in our final flesh.

BENIGN TUMOUR

Our first proper holiday after my operation –
'Partial debulking' is what they call it.
We were on the beach together. You needed to cross the estuary.
Watching the ferry approach I asked if you had the right change.
Then as I was saying goodbye it came,
That moment of indescribable strangeness
Called an 'aura'. It's as if a gear shifts in my brain
And I felt I was seeing you for the very first time
Where you were standing beside me on the sand.
It was the thing still lodged in my head
That appeared to be telling me this
As you climbed in the little boat and sailed away.
I stood there for some time in the hot sun.
I watched the glittering water
Not feeling altogether well
As if 'consciousness of self' were a sort of illness
And waiting there at the river's edge I was trying
So hard to remember
How, taking me by the hand, it had led me here.

SWIFT

Entered my room to a short-lived storm of wings.
How the swift got in there I do not know.
The window had been closed for hours.
Huddled there on the floor it looked up
Out of startled eyes, more animal than bird.
I opened the window and scooped the thing out
Like an insect. It sailed away,
Just a few ounces of flight this
Creature that's riskily other.
There's the way it consists of moments –
Wings and the benefit of air
Being so suddenly there, is one instant
In the afternoon-devouring emptiness.
What's *me* is something that's left
Hurtling around inside
As if I had swallowed self like an echo.
Now pressed against the window's ache of glass
It watches for that momentary return.

LAKE

Bending, at day's beginning,
Over my scraps I am Tantalus
Half-buried in my waters.
Two days before
There was that corrie lake we'd found,
Its silence so abruptly come upon,
The lisp and whisper at the black stone shore,
A sunless dazzle, something held and waiting.

I go out into September sunshine.
My face is hot one side and cold the other.
I walk to where the slabs of rock
Are tilted upward from the road.
It looks deliberately gardened
As if it has been waiting for me –
Honeysuckle, purple loosestrife
But all is on the fade as if
Seen in a mirror with a faint tarnish.
I turn, and watch
Today's inscrutable currents.
I strain to see you swimming to your island,
The one that you have chosen for today.
Your head's a mobile punctuation mark,
The trail you make a pale
Blemish in the water.
Now I have lost it, must imagine you
Pulling your body, seal-heavy, onto rock.

Returning home I'm at the window
Watching the sheet of quiet water
It's then I see you stretching upward –
You are unfolding in the distance like
A letter in a picture book.
Energetically you wave –
                        And me? I've had to turn away
To put the words down on my page of silence.

BREATHE, THEN

There's more good news says Tuka
The mirror is empty
                Tukaram, trans Dilip Chitre

'Come, little mouth', they'd said
'It is expedient to breathe'.
Unwinking the mirror's siege
It grew itself a shadow full of words,

An infant's pronoun-rapture, seized with self –
And somewhere else the world
Being violently named,
But now there are these patient afternoons,

As if the day were hiding from itself.
Going back to look it is as if
I cannot quite remember
Just where it was I'd left it

That day the blow fell, dreaming myself awake
To an existence in the light.
I find it coming home to me again
And now I may have reached a place

Where something fatal reaches me.
I am the reader moving up behind me
Who hovers like an afterthought.
There is the storyteller in my head –

The one who rises with those fallen eyes,
The me-not-me that I'm being spoken by.
This may be as far as I
Can take him with me now.

Creeping upstairs like a child perhaps I'll
Find him, thinking the sky
In a room where a mirror shallow with sunlight
Glosses the day. It empties. Outside

There is a single bird, its song
Intact, clouds wasting all the afternoon.
It will be almost the world
In there, as if that might be enough

To strengthen my faith in appearances
Arriving, word-perfect now
And, hearing something breathe itself, I'll breathe:
Imagine living here.

I IS

From 'he' to 'I' the pronoun –
It travelled the sky,
Being fathered: what I am heir to,
Tongue pressed against the moment,

I is
A mind simply
At play with itself

And this was where
The breathing found him
Who will be up early – an old man
He waits for the sun to rise.
Years later, and I am passing my hand
Over the stone face, asking forgiveness.

MIRRORED

Uncover this –
        being
it is a poor am.

We two, being
worded together

who are dusts on the mirror.

.

I thinks of you
Behind a window waiting
The sunlight winking back

Here being when
There is no more
Pronoun
      am
Being lifted up: one

Axe-bright moment

www.ingramcontent.com/pod-product-compliance
Lightning Source LLC
Chambersburg PA
CBHW032051150426
43194CB00006B/496